Carlisle United: A Season in the Sun
1974-75

DESERT ISLAND FOOTBALL HISTORIES

Carlisle United:

A Season in the Sun
1974-75

Series Editor: Clive Leatherdale
Series Consultant: Leigh Edwards

David Steele

DESERT ISLAND BOOKS

First published in 2006
by
DESERT ISLAND BOOKS LIMITED
7 Clarence Road, Southend-on-Sea, Essex SS1 1AN
United Kingdom
www.desertislandbooks.com

The right of David Steele to be identified as author of this work has been
asserted under The Copyright Designs and Patents Act 1988

British Library Cataloguing-in-Publication Data
A catalogue record for this book is available from the British Library

ISBN-13 978-1-905328-21-5
ISBN-10 1-905328-21-4

Printed in Great Britain
by
Biddles Ltd, King's Lynn

The publishers gratefully acknowledge Cumbrian Newspapers for the use of
all photographs in this book, with the exception of those featuring Luton Town.
These came from the Roger Wash collection

Thanks also to Donal Cullen for checking statistics

Contents

Author's Note

It was my Dad, Tom Steele, who first took me to see a Carlisle United match 50 years ago today, on 1 September 1956. Carlisle lost 1-2 to Southport but the experience must have struck a chord. Before long, I would go to Brunton Park as often as either he or my Uncle Alf would take me. In many ways, therefore, my Dad is the begetter of this work. Sadly, he died in 1994 but he did see Carlisle play in the First Division and I like to think he would have enjoyed this book.

I owe a great debt of gratitude to Vic Gibson of Cumbrian Newspapers for his support. This book would not have appeared in its current form without his help and that of his colleague Mike Gardner. I am also grateful to Paul Johnson for his assistance in preparing those photographs which are the copyright of Cumbrian Newspapers. I am also pleased to acknowledge their archive of match reports for the source of the bulk of the contemporary quotations.

My thanks are, of course, also due to the Carlisle United players of that era, without whom this book would never have been written. I have spoken to most of them, either in preparing this book or while researching articles over the years, and without exception all were very helpful to me. The late Allan Ross, in particular, was very astute in his observations and was always happy to give me the benefit of his thoughts and opinions on his time at Carlisle United. I am also grateful to Bill Green, the captain of the team, for agreeing to write the foreword to the book.

The staff at Carlisle Library have always been helpful whenever I have asked for any assistance and this book has involved many hours scrutinising microfilm copies of newspapers. More generally, I am grateful to Denis Easterby for his advice and support over the years, particularly as his memory extends back much further than mine.

I am grateful to my publisher Clive Leatherdale for affording me the opportunity to tell this story, which I hope will be a suitable tribute to the team and will recall some glorious memories for those who saw them in action. Thanks are also due to Leigh Edwards for recommending me to Clive and Desert Island Books.

Special thanks are due to my daughter Rachel who has been a great source of support and encouragement and in particular was always willing to help a computer illiterate such as myself. My final and greatest thanks, though, are due to my wife Joyce who has been a constant support, not just in the writing of this work but throughout the past 25 years. It is to her this book is dedicated.

DAVID STEELE
1 September 2006

Foreword

It was only on the intervention of the Hartlepool manager Len Ashurst that I got the opportunity to join Carlisle United in the summer of 1973. I was down in Swindon ready to put pen to paper, when I was informed that my 'Dad' was on the phone.

On taking the call, my 'Dad' turned out to be Len. Being unhappy with how Swindon had conducted the transfer – trying to sign me on the cheap – he was delighted to inform me that Carlisle had agreed a fee and that Alan Ashman would 'top' anything Swindon had offered. Plus there was the added bonus of a club house as well.

After a long train journey back to the North East, I drove over to Carlisle and was met by Hughie Neil, who took me to an allotment to meet Dick Young, who was feeding his pigeons. Later in the day I met Alan Ashman and quickly agreed terms (no agents). It was quite a step up for a young Fourth Division player to the Second Division.

It's funny how things turn out – in that first season Swindon were relegated, whilst 'Little Carlisle', as we all know achieved promotion to the First Division.

The strength of the team was its togetherness – only a small squad – all the players were on the same terms if in the first XI. Therefore there were no big egos – no cliques – just a desire to do well. The backroom staff were integral to the club's success. Dick Young's insistence on playing 'push and run' football was good on the eye. Hughie Neil was instrumental in bringing in players who could adapt to the 'Carlisle' way of playing. Alan Ashman was quiet – a thinker – but was able to give belief that we could affect the promotion race.

The success of the promotion season was particularly thrilling for the elder statesmen of the side – long-time servants Allan Ross and Chris Balderstone. They would never have believed when coming to Carlisle in the lower divisions that they would, in time, make the top one.

Once promotion was achieved everyone looked forward to the fixtures coming out. Chelsea at Stamford Bridge on the opening day. Now we believed it.

Everyone knows the outcome of the First Division campaign, but I really do believe that we brought something to the party – the reality that a 'small', well-run club can get amongst the 'Big Boys' – attractive passing football and some superb memories for many Cumbrians.

Wins away at Chelsea and Manchester City, home win v Spurs, home and away wins v Everton and three points taken off Derby County (champions) – who were demolished 3-0 at Brunton and held 0-0 at the Baseball Ground, plus an epic run in the FA Cup to the quarter-finals.

Other smaller clubs have trod the same path in later years, notably Wimbledon, Wigan, Reading, Barnsley etc, but it was Carlisle who proved it was possible and gave them the dream.

BILL GREEN

CHAPTER 1

Laying the Foundations

It was Bill Shankly who has provided perhaps the best-remembered assessment of Carlisle United's achievement in gaining promotion to the First Division in May 1974. In writing the introduction to *The Carlisle United Story* published in 1974 he stated that 'I would say it is the greatest feat in the history of the game, Carlisle United getting into the First Division of the English League'. Shankly of course was no stranger to hyperbole, particularly where he had a personal interest in the team or the player concerned. Yet though it was back in 1951 when he left Brunton Park on the managerial odyssey that would eventually take him via Grimsby, Workington and Huddersfield to Anfield and Liverpool FC eight years later, his connection with Carlisle United stretched back in a sense almost to the beginnings of the club.

It was in 1904 that the name of Carlisle United is first recorded. The AGM of Shaddongate United took place on 17 May and the most heated debate of the evening concerned the proposed change of name of the club from Shaddongate United to Carlisle United. Shaddongate were arguably the leading football club in the city at that time, although this claim might have been disputed by their local rivals, in particular Carlisle Red Rose.

The stated aim of the change was to try and develop a representative Carlisle team, and in this the proposal was successful. Carlisle United won both the Cumberland League and the Cumberland Cup in 1904-05, the first team to do this particular double. In furtherance of their ambitions they then applied to join the Second Division of the Lancashire Combination in 1905. Apart from Workington, who joined at the same time, the Combination was, as its name suggests, very much Lancashire based and for two seasons both Cumberland sides had to subsidise the travel expenses of the visiting teams. Carlisle United were an ambitious organisation and in 1906 they became a limited company issuing up to £2,000 in shares. The club's aim was promotion to the First Division of the Combination and among the new players signed in the 1906 close season were two recruits from Preston North End.

Billy Blyth was a Scot who had initially moved south to Portsmouth, where his elder brother Bob was a player. Bob stayed in the south but Billy moved north from Pompey to Preston. In April 1906 he made his solitary Football League appearance for North End at Sunderland. Davie

Maher was a Preston teammate of Blyth's and, though his career at Deepdale had been more successful, he too was persuaded to join the ambitious club in the Lancashire Combination.

Billy Blyth soon became the team captain and was almost certainly the most influential member of the side in the period prior to the First World War. For Carlisle United it was a period marked by a rapid rise to fame followed by an equally speedy fall from grace that almost put the club out of existence. In what was only their second season in the Combination, United won the Second Division championship in 1907. Promotion to the First Division of the Combination meant fixtures against the Reserve sides of the Merseyside pair of Everton and Liverpool, as well as Manchester City and United. The Cumbrians acquitted themselves well enough to finish as runners up in Division One behind Everton Reserves as well as reaching the FA Cup second round (the equivalent of today's fourth round).

Disaster though was not far behind this triumphant year and served as an early warning of the dangers of too rapid a rise. Carlisle United also ran a Reserve team of their own which played in the North Eastern League. Although games against the sides in the Lancashire Combination sides were popular with spectators, the Reserve team's fixtures were much less attractive and the costs of running this team soon became a drain upon the always fragile state of the club's finances. In the summer of 1909 the club moved from its old home at Devonshire Park to nearby Brunton Park and this was an additional expense the club had to bear. Twelve months later United decided to resign from the Lancashire Combination and instead to remain in the North Eastern League. Travel expenses would be lower, though it is also true to say that the Combination clubs were none too keen on having clubs as distant as Carlisle and Workington on their fixture list.

Financially the decision to concentrate on the North East was disastrous. By the summer of 1911 Carlisle United were bankrupt and the club secretary prepared to offer the club's resignation from the League. The club went into liquidation but remarkably the team survived. Most of the players approached the directors and offered to play for nothing until other expenses were met, and with this proviso Blyth and Carlisle United were able to continue, albeit at times with difficulty until the outbreak of the Great War in 1914.

Billy Blyth's own playing career ended at about this time but he remained in Carlisle, becoming in due course the manager of the Bowling Green Hotel in Lowther Street. He retained his connection with Carlisle United as well, eventually becoming a director of the club and later on the chairman. His elder brother Bob, incidentally, also attained a similar distinction at Portsmouth, although both men had to obtain special permission from the Football League to be allowed to progress, as it were, from the pitch to the boardroom.

As for Carlisle United, they resumed life in the North Eastern League in 1919. Two years later, some of its clubs, including Darlington and Hartlepool, as well as less obvious names such as Ashington and Durham City, applied to join the newly formed Third Division (North) of the Football League. Carlisle United, perhaps mindful of the financial disasters that had already befallen the club, decided this time on a more cautious approach, preferring instead to focus on buying the freehold of Brunton Park, an aim that was achieved in 1921. The following year the club won the North Eastern League title for the first and, as it transpired, only time but it was not until 1926 that the directors felt confident enough to apply to join the Football League. Two years later and at the third time of asking they were successful in the annual re-election ballot, taking the place of Durham City who thus returned to the North Eastern League.

Carlisle United began life in the Football League on 25 August 1928 with a 3-2 victory at Accrington Stanley. The Cumbrians finished eighth in that first season, thanks to a 42-goal contribution from centre-forward Jimmy McConnell, a tally that remains a club record for League goals in a season. That first season was in many ways the club's most successful campaign in the pre-war era. As ever, financial problems were never far away and by the spring of 1932 the club was again close to bankruptcy until a special friendly match against Cup winners Newcastle United brought a much-needed injection of funds to the club.

In was in this context that Bill Shankly first arrived at Carlisle United in August 1932. His four elder brothers had all become professional footballers and one of them had already had a spell at Brunton Park. Jimmy Shankly had signed for Carlisle in 1926, on one occasion scoring seven goals in a North Eastern League game before moving to Sheffield United, Southend and Barrow. Moreover, Shankly's mother Barbara was the sister of Billy Blyth and it was no doubt partly through this connection that the eighteen-year-old Shankly travelled down to Carlisle from his Ayrshire home on a month's trial. His debut for the Reserve side ended in a 0-6 defeat but despite this reverse he was immediately offered terms by the club. After several months in the Reserves, he made his League debut for Carlisle on the last day of 1932 in a 2-2 draw against Rochdale. By the end of the 1932-33 season, he had made sixteen appearances for the Cumbrians in the Third Division (North) but despite his efforts the club had finished the season in nineteenth place, one rung below the previous term. The idea that Carlisle United might one day play in the First Division in their own right must have seemed at the time incredible.

Most of the Carlisle team were released in the 1933 close season but the young Shankly was offered terms for another year. He accepted but then the club received an offer of £500 from Preston North End, then in the Second Division, for his services. To a cash-strapped club such as Carlisle, this sum was too good to turn down. Though the young Shankly was not initially minded to accept, especially when he learned that his personal terms would be little better than at Carlisle, eventually he did so and moved to Deepdale where he would spend the remainder of his playing career, winning an FA Cup medal in 1938 as well as five caps for Scotland.

Carlisle United, meanwhile, remained in the Third Division (North) and, though they only once had to suffer the indignity of seeking re-election, nor was there any evidence that they would ever rise even to the dizzy heights of the Second Division. Not that they would have encountered Shankly and Preston North End there in any case. His new club were promoted back into the First Division in 1934 and Shankly was to play at that level for the rest of his career at Deepdale.

The outbreak of the Second World War in September 1939 put an end to the Football League for the next seven years. When normal football life finally resumed in August 1946, Carlisle United began by appointing a 23-year-old as the club's new player-manager. Ivor Broadis had been posted to nearby Crosby aerodrome at the end of the war. He was a Londoner and had been on Tottenham's books in 1939 but had guested for other clubs during the war. Finding that he enjoyed life in Carlisle, where incidentally he still resides, he was offered the post of player manager when he was demobbed in 1946. The club's chairman at the time was Billy Blyth.

As ever, Carlisle United were being run on the proverbial shoestring. The ground possessed the one old grandstand that had originally been brought to Brunton Park in 1909 when the club moved from its previous home in nearby Devonshire Park. As Shankly later recalled, it was little more than a glorified hencoop.

The club had little money but gradually some progress was made and in 1948 United finished in ninth position in the table, the best performance since 1928. Meanwhile the pace and shooting power of Broadis himself was beginning to attract the attention of bigger clubs. In January 1949, in a unique transaction, Broadis in effect transferred himself to

Sunderland for a fee of £18,000, which was a record for a Third Division (North) club.

At last Carlisle United had some money in the bank as they advertised for a new manager. At Deepdale, meanwhile, Bill Shankly was nearing the end of his playing career and keen to move into management. He applied for the job and despite losing the prospect of a benefit that had been due to him by Preston, took over the managerial reins at Brunton Park in April 1949.

The Shankly era lasted just two years at Carlisle but it remains among the most memorable managerial spells at Brunton Park and not just because of his subsequent fame and fortune at Anfield. One of his first acts was to burn the old communal training kit and to replace it with new clothing. With the transfer money he was allocated he made some shrewd signings, many of them fellow Scots, such as McIntosh at full-back, Kinloch at half-back and Jackson and McCue among the forwards. Right-winger Billy Hogan arrived from Manchester City and Paddy Waters, who had been capped by Ireland, joined from Preston North End. Most of these players became United stalwarts for several years even after Shankly had moved on.

The 1950-51 season saw the club rise to third place in the table, setting a new club record of fifteen matches unbeaten at one point. It was the only time between 1928 and 1965 that United looked to have any real chance of promotion to the Second Division, and the final points total of 62 would in some years have been sufficient to win a Third Division title. In January 1951 Carlisle travelled to Highbury to do battle with Cup-holders Arsenal in the third round of the FA Cup. It was the first time since 1910 that United had played in the capital but it proved to be an occasion well worth the wait. Before a crowd of 57,932, still the second biggest gate to watch any Carlisle match, United held Arsenal to a 0-0 draw. For Shankly, who reputedly had his own reasons for wanting to put one over on Arsenal after he was omitted from their side in a wartime Cup final, it was an almost unalloyed triumph. His unheralded charges dominated the game and were unlucky not to win the tie. They returned home to a crowd of thousands gathered outside the railway station.

The replay at Brunton Park was lost 1-4, though not before Carlisle equalised, while the Arsenal full-back saved another certain goal with his fist. Yet despite these days of glory, Shankly had made up his mind that, as in 1933, he would have to move on to further his ambitions. At the end of the 1950-51 season it was announced that he had taken up the manager's post at Grimsby Town, a club that had themselves just been relegated to the Third Division (North), although only four years earlier they had been a First Division side. In terms of size, Grimsby is not that much bigger than Carlisle, but there was no doubting his new club's footballing pedigree, which included more than a decade in Division One, as well as an FA Cup semi-final appearance in 1939. Although the Mariners have never subsequently returned to the First Division, in 1951 they must have seemed a far better bet to reach the top flight than Carlisle United.

Shankly's successor as manager was Fred Emery, who for the previous eight years had occupied the managerial chair at Bradford Park Avenue. Though born in Lincoln, the bulk of his playing career had been as a half-back with Doncaster Rovers, for whom he still holds the club's appearance record. One of his first acts as manager was to break his new club's transfer record by signing centre-forward Alan Ashman from Nottingham Forest.

Alan Ashman had, rather auspiciously, been born in the same week in 1928 that saw Carlisle United elected to the Football League. He had made his League debut with Forest in 1949 after his National Service but was to make only a handful of first-team appearances at the City ground. Ashman is generally regarded, and rightly so, as the most successful manager the club has ever had and it is easy to overlook the fact that he is also among the most prolific goalscorers in Carlisle's history. Making his debut in August 1951 against Rochdale, he became the first and only Carlisle player to score a hat-trick on his first appearance for the club. Ashman was especially effective in the air and this forte was complemented a few weeks later when Jimmy Whitehouse joined the club. 'Wham' Whitehouse was blessed with a powerful shot and for some years Carlisle's standard attacking technique was a long ball or a cross to Ashman who would nod it down for Whitehouse to shoot at goal.

Alan Ashman and Jimmy Whitehouse both netted over 100 League and Cup goals for Carlisle. In fact, despite his own position at half-back, Fred Emery is perhaps best remembered for bringing talented forwards such as Ashman, Whitehouse and later Alf 'Ack Ack' Ackerman to Brunton Park. In 1955 Ivor Broadis also returned to the club as player-coach but in 1958 Carlisle ended their final season in the Third Division (North) in fourteenth place. As a result, the club became founder members of the new Fourth Division and Fred Emery was dismissed as manager. His replacement as United's new boss was Andy Beattie. Once a playing colleague of Bill Shankly at Preston, Beattie was formerly the manager of, among other clubs, Huddersfield Town where Shanks had succeeded him in the post in 1956.

By the time Andy Beattie arrived at Brunton Park, the careers of both Ashman and Whitehouse were coming to an end, while Ivor Broadis was also in the twilight of his playing days. There was, though, another even more significant addition to the Brunton Park staff who had arrived at the club two years earlier.

Dick Young was born in 1918 and grew up in the North East. A career in football offered him the chance to escape going down the pit and in 1935 he was signed by Sheffield United. Like many of his generation the war robbed him of his best years in football but he returned to Bramhall Lane when hostilities ended, later moving to Lincoln City. He eventually became player-coach at Sincil Bank where Tony Emery, the nephew of Fred, was the first-team centre-half. Through him he learned that Carlisle United were looking for a full-time trainer. Although it meant a step down from Second Division Lincoln, Dick applied and in 1956 arrived at the Brunton Park ground where he would spend the rest of his career.

Dick Young never kicked a ball in anger for Carlisle United yet his contribution to the club and its later success was as great as many of those who played on the park. He was a great believer in making the ball do the work. 'The ball is round, push it around' was one of his mantras. He expected players to work on their ball skills and would certainly have approved of golfer Gary Player's remark after playing a supposedly lucky shot that 'the more I practise, the luckier I get'. Throughout his time at the club, a host of players were to arrive and leave as better footballers than when they came. The greatest credit for this belongs to Dick Young.

After Andy Beattie left in 1960, he was replaced by Ivor Powell. Under him, Carlisle achieved their first ever promotion, rising from Division Four in May 1962 by beating Chester in the last game of the season. It was a short-lived triumph and in January 1963 he was dismissed after the club lost at home to non-league Gravesend & Northfleet in the FA Cup. By this time, Carlisle were also facing almost certain relegation back to Division Four. His successor meanwhile was already a familiar figure to United fans.

When Alan Ashman's playing career ended, he became a chicken farmer working for Jim Monkhouse who was also a Carlisle director. Ashman also took over as the manager of Penrith, who played in the Northern League. In his four years there, he piloted Penrith from the bottom of the league to second from top, as well as guiding them to their best ever run in the Amateur Cup.

Arriving at Brunton Park in the throes of one of the worst winters of the century, with the club facing almost certain relegation, his immediate inheritance must have seemed bleak. The suggestion that Brunton Park would one day host First Division football would have been viewed with ridicule, had anyone been rash enough to suggest it. Yet within four months he had recruited two of the players who would feature in Carlisle's First Division campaign little over a decade later.

Alan Ashman returned to his home town of Rotherham for his first signing. Hugh McIlmoyle had hit the national headlines in May 1961 when Leicester City chose him to play in their FA Cup final team after just seven first-team appearances. Leicester lost the final to Spurs, who thus clinched their historic League and Cup double. Within a year, Hugh McIlmoyle had been transferred to Rotherham United in Division Two where Ashman had heard that the young Scot was not very settled. Like Ashman himself, Hugh McIlmoyle was an outstanding header of the ball, though his future manager reputedly never saw him play before signing him in March 1963. Hugh McIlmoyle scored twice on his debut for Carlisle, inspiring a rare home win as Notts Co were defeated 4-2.

One of United's more valuable assets at the time was a full-back who was coveted by Second Division Luton Town. A deal was agreed for Alex McBain to be exchanged for Luton winger Jack Lornie but, rather than a cash adjustment, Luton preferred to offer Carlisle one of their reserves. Goalkeeper Allan Ross impressed the visiting United delegation sufficiently to be chosen as the makeweight in the deal. Jack Lornie only played four games for Carlisle and Alex McBain spent just two years at Kenilworth Road. Allan Ross, however, went on to become Carlisle's record appearance holder and was the only United player to remain at the club throughout the rise from the Fourth Division to the First.

Alan Ashman was aware that luck played its part, Gary Player's dictum notwithstanding, in football management. 'I knew Hugh McIlmoyle was good but I did not know he was that good,' he once mused years later as Hugh McIlmoyle scored 44 League and Cup goals in the 1963-64 campaign. He was the country's leading scorer as Carlisle netted a club record 113 goals. How ironic, then, that they lost the Fourth Division championship to Gillingham on goal-average, despite scoring almost twice as many goals as the men from Kent.

Yet twelve months later, United and Ashman went one better as the club clinched the Third Division title by beating rivals Mansfield 3-0 in the final match of the campaign at Brunton Park. This was despite the sale of Hugh McIlmoyle to First Division Wolves for a club record £30,000 in the autumn of 1964. Allan Ross was gradually establishing himself as the club's first-choice goalkeeper, though for some time he shared duty between the posts with fellow keeper Joe Dean. Meanwhile, the 1965 close season saw the arrival of another future First Division player to Brunton Park.

Chris Balderstone came from Huddersfield where he attended the same school as Willie Watson some twenty years earlier. Watson eventually became a double international, winning four England football caps while playing for Sunderland, as well as representing England in 23 Test matches. Balderstone showed similar promise, representing the town's Schoolboys at both football and cricket before joining the ground staff at Huddersfield Town, whose manager by then was Bill Shankly. His League debut came in March 1959, taking the place of the injured Denis Law in Town's Second Division game at Cardiff. Chris scored his team's only goal and by early 1965 had made well over 100 first-team appearances for the Terriers. His cricket career, too, was progressing and he made his Yorkshire debut in June 1961 reaching that milestone earlier than his contemporary Geoffrey Boycott.

Football, though, was his premier sport at that time but early in 1965 he lost his place in the Huddersfield Town team. Playing for the Reserves in an end of season game, Dick Young saw him 'spraying the ball about as though he had invented the game'. In May 1965 a £7,000 fee brought Chris Balderstone to Brunton Park as United prepared for their first ever season in Division Two.

The campaign opened with United entertaining Norwich City. After two minutes it was Balderstone who put Carlisle ahead and the Cumbrians ran out 4-1 winners. It was their home form that kept Carlisle in Division Two in the first season, as the club lost its opening thirteen games away from Brunton Park. Despite only one away victory all season, the final position of fourteenth was a very satisfactory beginning. Chris Balderstone was top scorer with thirteen goals, though for Allan Ross it was a campaign spent almost entirely in the Reserves, his sole first-team appearance coming in an FA Cup-tie.

The following term saw Carlisle rise to third place in the table, assisted by a good run of results at the end of the season. In those days only two clubs were promoted to Division One, nor were there any play-offs. Yet to have guided the Cumbrians from the depths of the Fourth Division to the brink of the top flight in just over four seasons was a measure of the achievement of Alan Ashman, Dick Young and the playing staff at Brunton Park. In fact, the club's total of 52 points was three higher than the 49 they would amass seven years later in their successful promotion to Division One.

One of United's last away matches in the 1966-67 season was a 3-3 draw at Northampton Town. Carlisle had already beaten the Cobblers at Brunton Park and at the end of that season Town were relegated to Division Three. Two seasons after that they were back in the Fourth, which they had left a decade earlier in their famous rise to Division One. By the time the two clubs again found themselves in the same division, Carlisle too would have completed the same journey as the Cobblers, although for Carlisle both the rise and fall were somewhat more gradual.

For the next five years, however, Carlisle United would be under different management. In May 1967 it was announced that Alan Ashman would be leaving Brunton Park to take over at West Bromwich Albion. He perhaps felt that he had taken Carlisle as far as he could and certainly he had taken them a lot further than anyone could reasonably have expected. Albion were an established First Division club who had finished the season in mid-table. In Alan Ashman's first year there he led the Baggies to FA Cup success, beating favourites Everton 1-0 in the final. Nearly 40 years later, it remains the last major addition to the club's trophy cabinet. Two years later West Brom returned to Wembley, losing the League Cup final 1-2 to Manchester City, but success in the League continued to elude them. In May 1971 Arsenal clinched their first League and Cup double, emulating the feat of Tottenham Hotspur ten years earlier. Central to their achievement was the coaching of Don Howe, the former West Brom and England full-back. He was invited to take over as manager at the Hawthorns as Alan Ashman suffered the fate of almost all those who choose to manage a football club.

To revert back to 1967, Alan Ashman's successor at Brunton Park was Tim Ward. Ward was a former England international who had previously managed Barnsley and then Derby County, where he had made way for Brian Clough. Tim Ward was one of nature's gentlemen and in his only full season at Brunton Park United finished just above halfway in the table. In addition, the club notched up a famous FA Cup victory at Newcastle. The following season, however, began in disastrous fashion and Tim Ward paid the inevitable price.

His successor was Bob Stokoe who had been the boss at Rochdale and before that at Charlton and Bury, where his managerial career had begun. Bob Stokoe too was a gentleman but of a different stamp to his predecessor. Making a strong defence a priority, he turned Carlisle's season around with a series of low-scoring victories, interspersed with the occasional goalless draw. Hugh McIlmoyle had returned to Brunton Park during Tim Ward's reign and Stokoe made him captain. In the 1969-70 campaign, the board took the controversial decision to sell McIlmoyle for a second time; this time it was Middlesbrough who wrote the £55,000 cheque. Despite the sale, Carlisle embarked on their most successful League Cup run before losing to Alan Ashman's West Bromwich Albion in the semi-final. For a number of Carlisle's older players, the defeat by

West Brom marked the virtual end of their Brunton Park careers, as Stokoe sought to rebuild the side. A year later he too was on his way, this time to Blackpool, whom he joined as their new manager at the end of 1970.

Ian McFarlane was the new man at Carlisle's helm. He had been a coach at Middlesbrough and then Manchester City, following a relatively modest playing career. Inheriting a stronger squad than his predecessor, Carlisle finished fourth in 1970-71, falling to tenth place in the following season. McFarlane is probably best remembered for resurrecting the career of Stan Bowles, who had once been sacked by Manchester City and whom McFarlane bought from Crewe for a bargain £12,000. Among the most naturally gifted players ever to pull on a Carlisle United shirt, the club made a profit of almost £100,000, when he was sold to Queens Park Rangers less than a year later.

By then, McFarlane himself had been dismissed, for reasons that still remain mysterious, in May 1972. Speculation as ever centred round his replacement, not least because of the possible availability of Alan Ashman, who had taken over at Olympiakos of Athens following his dismissal from West Brom. Nor was this the only issue to be resolved by the Brunton Park directors, as for the first time ever Carlisle United had qualified for a European competition. The Anglo-Italian Competition may not have had the resonance of the European Cup but for United fans it afforded a rare chance to see their team play on a continental stage.

CHAPTER 2

Alan Ashman Returns

In mid-March 1972 it was announced that Carlisle United would be taking part in the Anglo-Italian Tournament to be held in the first fortnight of June. 'The biggest thing which has ever happened to the fans here' was the immediate verdict of United boss Ian McFarlane, little realising that he would not be the manager by the time the tournament was due to begin. His verdict on the role of the tournament in the club's history was also open to question, notwithstanding the significance of the event. In fact, the first ever foreign visitors to Brunton Park were a Dutch amateur side as far back as 1909, while the 1950s and 1960s had seen the occasional visit by continental opponents for friendly matches. Yet the very fact that United had been invited to compete was a further measure of the progress that the club had been making.

Only a handful of the club's playing staff had any first-hand experience of Italian football. One of the few who had was full-back John Gorman who had travelled there with the Celtic Youth team some years earlier. The tournament itself was in its third year and in 1972 involved eight teams from each country, which were broken down into four mini-leagues. Each team played a total of four games that comprised home and away fixtures against the two teams from the other country. Points were awarded not just for wins (2 points) and draws (1 point) but an additional point was earned for every goal scored.

Meanwhile, the regular League season ended for Carlisle at a wet Loftus Road on 29 April 1972 where they lost 0-4 to Queens Park Rangers. Normally this would have signalled a break of two months or so before the need to report back for pre-season training in early July. This time the players were able to disperse for barely a fortnight before returning to Brunton Park. For captain Chris Balderstone it was particularly frustrating as his opportunities to play cricket during the summer break would be even more curtailed than usual. At this stage, however, football was still his sporting priority, though not as it turned out for very much longer.

Yet for those remaining at Brunton Park during this period, there was no lack of incident. The end of April saw right-back Steve Derrett signed from Cardiff City. He was a Welsh international and thus became the only full international on the club's books. In fact, one of those five caps had been earned against Italy in the Olympic Stadium in Rome. A few

days later Les O'Neill arrived from Bradford City, who had just been relegated to the Fourth Division. He was a one-time Newcastle trainee who
after a single appearance for the Magpies had plied his trade in the lower
divisions with Darlington and then the Bantams, racking up a total of
almost 300 League appearances for the two clubs.

With his international pedigree, as well as his experience at Second
Division Cardiff City, it might have been supposed that Steve Derrett
would have had the greater impact on United's fortunes. In the event, he
made barely a dozen appearances at Brunton Park before eventually joining Rotherham in December 1973. Les O'Neill, meanwhile, proved to be
an exceptional signing for the club, where he would remain for the rest
of his playing career. A consistent and hardworking performer in midfield, as either provider or goalscorer, he was to prove an integral member of the Carlisle United First Division side.

Photos of the two recruits alongside the United manager had no
sooner appeared in the local press before it was announced that Ian
McFarlane had been relieved of his duties. He had been at the club for
just a season and a half, and to most observers he had acquitted himself
well in terms of the club's performances. United had finished in tenth
place in the season just ended as well as holding First Division Tottenham
to a draw in the FA Cup. Moreover, in reviving the career of the extrav-
agantly gifted Stan Bowles, he had earned himself the gratitude not just
of United fans but also of anyone in England who appreciated footballing skills of the highest order. Officially his dismissal was due to his
inability to run a one-team system, combined with a lack of experience,
but if the true reasons for his abrupt departure were other than this, they
have never been made public.

With the forthcoming venture to Italy fast approaching, the club
announced that Dick Young would act as caretaker manager and be in
charge for the Italian job. After sixteen years at the club, acting as trainer
and coach to no fewer than seven different managers, nobody could
argue that he was not due his opportunity to show how he could perform
in the managerial role. Meanwhile, any speculation that Alan Ashman
could be returning to Brunton Park was firmly rebutted by the club who
stated they were in no hurry to appoint a replacement for the departed
Ian McFarlane.

The players duly reassembled in mid-May and after friendly matches
at Workington and Kendal the sixteen-man squad flew to Italy on 30 May.
The draw had paired Carlisle with Stoke City and the two clubs were each
scheduled to play against AS Roma and Catanzaro. Roma had just finished seventh in the sixteen-team Serie 'A' and as regular participators in

European competitions boasted an array of international talent, although the two biggest names were both by now at the veteran stage. Luis Del Sol had been inside-right in the Real Madrid team that defeated Eintracht Frankfurt 7-3 in the 1960 European Cup final at Hampden Park, a game often regarded as the finest match ever played in Britain. Two years later Brazil retained the World Cup in Chile. Deputising for the injured Pele in the final was Amarildo who duly scored the first of Brazil's three goals against the Czechs.

Despite their foreign provenance, both Del Sol and Amarildo had played the bulk of their club football in Italy and in fact, at the age of 37, Del Sol was the oldest player in the Italian League. Catanzaro in contrast had made history of a different sort twelve months earlier by becoming the first team from the far south of Italy to play in Serie 'A'. Sadly they had finished second from bottom in their own 'season in the sun' and were duly relegated but in common with Carlisle United this was their first experience of a European competition.

Carlisle United opened their campaign on 1 June against Roma in the Olympic Stadium and caused a considerable upset by defeating the Italian giants 3-2. Those lucky enough to witness this event regard it as one of the finest performances in the club's history, the winning goal coming from a header by centre-half 'Tot' Winstanley. Three days later, before a crowd of just 3,000, Stan Bowles scored the only goal of the game as United won their second match of the tournament at Catanzaro. Among the other English clubs, Blackpool too had won their two matches but Stoke City, though also victorious in Catanzaro, had gone down against Roma.

United had calculated that a combined gate of 16,000 would be required for the two home matches in order to break even on the whole enterprise. The first game at Brunton Park, in which the opponents were Roma, attracted a gate of 12,000. This was despite the absence of both Del Sol and Amarildo who presumably felt no need to add Brunton Park to the list of great stadia in which they had performed. The game ended in a 3-3 draw, with Carlisle relinquishing a 3-1 lead. Three days later United completed their fixtures by overcoming Catanzaro 4-1 before a crowd of 8,153. With three wins and a draw, Carlisle had collected seven points plus a further eleven for goals scored. It was an impressive performance but Bob Stokoe's Blackpool won all four matches and aided by a 10-0 win in their final group game easily topped the league of English teams with 26 points. Roma rather surprisingly proved to be the leading Italian side with a modest fourteen points but then proceeded to defeat the Seasiders 3-0 in the final played in their Olympic Stadium.

By now, however, the focus for Carlisle fans was again on events at Brunton Park. On the day of the home tie with Roma it was announced that Alan Ashman would be returning to the club as manager. In his year in Greece, he had taken Olympiakos to third place in the First Division and qualification for the UEFA Cup, but despite taking a cut in the £25,000 salary he had been earning in Athens, the lure of Carlisle was clearly too great to resist.

Though the playing staff had inevitably seen many changes in the five years since he had moved to West Bromwich Albion, the backroom staff at Brunton Park had stayed remarkably constant throughout that period. EG (George) Sheffield had been a director since 1958 and chairman of the board for much of that time. The scion of a family of local landowners, he was a well-respected figure both inside and outside the club. Nor was he the only familiar figure in the boardroom. Seven of the club's nine directors had been in post when Ashman had left in 1967, as was the club secretary David Dent. He had been the youngest to hold such a post in the whole Football League when he was given the job in 1960 at the age of 23. He was to remain at the club until 1978 before moving to Coventry City and eventually to be appointed Secretary of the Football League. Dick Young, who had proved a more than capable caretaker manager during his month in charge, was of course a familiar figure as was physiotherapist Herbert Nicholson, another long-standing servant of the club. Hugh Neil had joined United in 1961, forming a successful full-back combination with Terry Caldwell. As players with contrasting styles, they complemented each other in their play but when injury brought Hugh Neil's career to a premature end, he joined the backroom staff, becoming in due course the club's chief scout.

As for the players that he inherited, the most familiar faces were Allan Ross and Chris Balderstone, both of whom had by now made some 300 appearances for the club. They were the sole survivors among the playing staff from five years earlier, though Dennis Martin was the one other player to be reunited with his former manager. Dennis was a skilful winger/inside-forward who was Alan Ashman's first signing for West Brom and spent three years at the Hawthorns before moving north to Brunton Park in the 1970 close season. The remaining players had all been recruited by Ashman's various predecessors but already the nucleus of the team that would win promotion in two years time was in place. In addition, Carlisle had begun under Bob Stokoe to adopt the one-team squad system of eighteen or nineteen players but with no reserve side.

Allan Ross was still first-choice goalkeeper but by now his deputy was Tom Clarke who had come down from Airdrie two years earlier. The outstanding full-back on the club's books was left-back John Gorman who had just been voted the club's first ever Player of the Year. He had been signed from Celtic two seasons earlier and was both a skilful defender and a full-back who loved to attack down the flank. He was still only 22 and had been ever-present in the campaign just ended. Derek Hemstead was the regular right-back and a veteran of almost 350 appearances for Carlisle and before that Scunthorpe, who were his only previous club. A fearless defender, sadly a ligament injury would end his career early into the following season.

Stan Ternent had, like John Gorman, been ever-present in the term just ended. A defender who took no prisoners, as the saying goes, his career too would eventually end prematurely through injury. Graham 'Tot' Winstanley had, in common with Les O'Neill, begun his career with Newcastle United before moving across the Pennines to Brunton Park in the autumn of 1969. A versatile central defender, he was to remain at the club just long enough to play in the First Division. In midfield, Frank Barton had been the third ever-present in 1971-72. Converted with great success by Bob Stokoe from a forward into a midfielder, he would follow his former boss to Blackpool before many weeks were out. Ray Train had also begun life as a forward with Walsall before coming north to Carlisle just six months earlier.

The top scorers for United in the season just ended were Bobby Owen and Stan Bowles. Bobby Owen had been a big-money signing by Manchester City when he joined them from Bury but had never really settled at Maine Road before coming to Carlisle. A consistent goalscorer throughout his career, I can still recall one of his most spectacular efforts as, with his back to goal, he lobbed the ball over his head and that of a Charlton defender before racing round and crashing the ball home with one of his trademark volleys. Stan Bowles had also been at Maine Road before being sacked from the club. He too had also played for Bury and later Crewe before coming to Brunton Park in the previous October for an absolute bargain fee of £12,000. One of the most gifted footballers of his generation, he was also the club's most obviously saleable asset and was about to be voted runner up to Birmingham's Trevor Francis in a Second Division Player of the Year poll.

Having narrowly missed promotion to Division One in his previous spell at the club, there is no doubt that Alan Ashman was seen by many as the man who could go one better than five years earlier. Promotion from Division Two was still two up and two down from the top flight, although at the Football League's AGM a proposal to change to three up and three down had been unsuccessfully proposed.

Ashman was understandably keen to play down expectations as he sought to get his feet back under the table at Brunton Park. An early success was to persuade Derek Hemstead to come off the transfer list and to remain at Carlisle. This left Frank Barton as the only player actively seeking a move and in July he was reunited with Bob Stokoe at Blackpool in exchange for a £20,000 fee. This deal took place just a few days after Ashman's own first venture into the transfer market to sign Joe Laidlaw from Middlesbrough. Laidlaw was a damaging and strong running forward who had already spent five seasons at Boro and he would prove to be one of the manager's most successful signings in his second spell at Brunton Park.

The pre-season friendlies began with a 2-0 win at Fourth Division Darlington. Four days later Carlisle entertained Stoke City, holders of the League Cup and the other English team in the Anglo-Italian Tournament who had encountered Roma and Catanzaro. Stoke City at that time were managed by Tony Waddington and he was never afraid to recruit stars who other clubs might have considered past their prime. The line up for the Potters that evening included two of England's World Cup heroes in Gordon Banks and Geoff Hurst. For Banks it was a rare chance to return to the ground where he had played at the very start of his career, for Chesterfield in an FA Cup-tie back in 1958. Geoff Hurst had only just joined Stoke City after his thirteen-year career with West Ham had come to an end and, so far as I am aware, this was the only time he trod the turf at Brunton Park.

The game attracted an above-average crowd of 8,341 for this encounter that ended in a 3-3 draw. The final goal came from a Stan Ternent free-kick which he curled round the defensive wall in the manner of David Beckham to beat the great England goalkeeper. The final friendly fixture resulted in a 2-3 defeat at Dumbarton who had just been promoted to the Scottish First Division. One of the Scottish team's goals was netted by a part-time joiner called Kenny Wilson who was a prolific scorer north of the border in his two years at Boghead Park. Nor was this the last time that Kenny Wilson would feature in the annals of Carlisle United.

United travelled to Burnley for their opening League fixture on 9 August 1972. The crowd of 9,804 was, perhaps surprisingly, the lowest at Turf Moor all season, as Carlisle fielded just one new player in Joe Laidlaw. Carlisle twice took the lead through Dennis Martin and Bobby Owen but had at the end to be content with a share of the spoils. With hindsight it was one of United's better performances of the season as by early September three consecutive victories had put Burnley top of the table, a position they would retain almost continuously for the remainder of the campaign. Seven days later Carlisle's home programme began with a 3-0 win over Swindon, though the 7,747 gate was seen as disappointing. A month later only 5,911 passed through the Brunton Park turnstiles to witness a 4-0 defeat of Cardiff City. It was the club's second lowest crowd in eight seasons of Second Division football, the lowest also being for a visit from Cardiff three years earlier.

Earlier that month Liverpool had travelled to Brunton Park for a second round League Cup-tie. Then, as now, Liverpool were a major footballing power, though they had not won anything since the League title six years earlier. The game attracted a crowd of 16,257 which, though considerable, was again seen by some as disappointing, especially as the tie was not all-ticket. Kevin Keegan, on his first visit to Brunton Park, put his side in the lead before Les O'Neill came off the bench to equalise.

The player whom Les replaced that night was Stan Bowles who was making his last appearance for United. The club had already turned down one bid of £100,000 from Crystal Palace but it was Queens Park Rangers who paid out the sum of £110,000 to secure his services. Stan Bowles had spent only ten months in Carlisle but it was long enough for him to demonstrate his rehabilitation as a player of the highest class. By the end of that 1972-73 season he had inspired Rangers to second place in the table and a return to the First Division where they had briefly played four years earlier.

The sale of Bowles meant that for once a Carlisle manager had some money to spend on a major signing. Defeat at Preston towards the end of September pushed United well below halfway in the table but two days later it was announced that Kenny Wilson had signed from Dumbarton for a record fee for both clubs of £36,000. Wilson had been a scoring sensation in the Scottish Second Division. Having been released by St Johnstone, he had been snapped up by Dumbarton whom he repaid with a total of over 80 goals in his two seasons at Boghead Park. His goals inspired the Sons to the Second Division title and, on the face of it, his fee looked good value for such a prolific goalscorer.

Things were looking brighter in other ways as well, as new floodlights were installed at Brunton Park. The old lights were thought to be worth a goal start to Carlisle United, so indifferent were they, but the new ones were considered state of the art. Needless to say it was not United who first benefited. Blackpool, managed by ex-United boss Bob Stokoe, ran out 3-2-winners the night they were formally switched on.

Kenny Wilson made a quiet debut against Blackpool but the team as a whole was not firing on all cylinders. A 0-4 defeat by QPR and Stan

Bowles at Loftus Road pushed Carlisle into the bottom three in the table as results away from home were proving difficult. Defeat at Orient two weeks later simply compounded this problem. The Orient match saw the first appearance of Brian Tiler, another player whose roots lay in Ashman's home town of Rotherham. Tiler had been made captain when Tommy Docherty had taken over as manager of Rotherham United and when the Doc moved to Aston Villa he took Brian Tiler with him. Tiler was a confident individual who adapted well to his new club both on and off the pitch and was ever present for the rest of the campaign.

Gradually United's fortunes revived, aided by a spell of four wins and a draw in five matches. The highlight of these encounters was undoubtedly a 4-3 victory over Sunderland, with Stan Ternent scoring a late winner after the Cumbrians had surrendered a 3-1 lead. Nobody could have guessed that eight of that Sunderland side, in the middle of a nine-game run without a win and lying close to the relegation places, would be celebrating the most unlikely FA Cup triumph of the century only six months later.

As the Wearsiders struggled, Carlisle's results continued to improve as 1972 drew to a close. Brighton and Hove Albion were thrashed 5-1 in mid-December with three of the goals coming from Bobby Owen. He thus briefly became the division's second highest scorer, as well as the source of the club's only hat-trick of the campaign. The Seagulls' consolation goal came courtesy of an Eddie Spearritt penalty. Eighteen months later he would be one of United's new signings as they prepared to face life in Division One. On Boxing Day Hugh McIlmoyle, who was also destined to feature in the Division One campaign, had an unhappy return to Brunton Park as his Preston team went down 6-1. Even Kenny Wilson, newly recovered from his own ligament injury, got his name on the scoresheet in that game. It proved to be the only time he did so in his spell at Brunton Park but by the end of the year Carlisle United were reasonably placed in mid-table. Off the pitch too, the club was in a healthy state as a profit of £82,000 was announced, including a £16,000 contribution from the supporters club.

Operating just a single team with a relatively modest squad meant that the club could be vulnerable to injury crises. Derek Hemstead's ligament damage was such that he never played again after the Nottingham Forest match in September. Stan Ternent was already suffering from the knee problems that would also curtail his career while Steve Derrett was another defender who was not always available. The signing of Peter Carr in November did, however, mean that the right-back problem was now solved. Carr was only 21 but already a veteran of well over 100 League games for Darlington. Blessed with pace and a positive approach to his defensive duties, he was the ideal foil to the silkier skills of John Gorman on the other flank and both players were almost ever present for the remainder of the season. With a combined age of only 44, the pairing was also obviously one for the future.

The New Year dawned with successive Saturday visits from Huddersfield Town, first in the League and then in the FA Cup. Both games ended all-square, as had United's League visit to Leeds Road back in the previous August. The deadlock was broken during the Cup replay in bizarre fashion. A speculative Kenny Wilson overhead kick was going wide until it cannoned off a startled Terry Dolan and the Huddersfield defender was 'credited' with the own-goal that decided the outcome. Carlisle's next match was a home tie with Sheffield United of the First Division.

Though weakened by the absence of the cup-tied Peter Carr and the suspended Joe Laidlaw, Carlisle pulled off a famous 2-1 victory to reach the fifth round for only the third time in the club's history. The winning goal came from a close-range effort from centre-half Bob Delgado. Delgado had been another Ian McFarlane signing and though his best position was in central defence, he acquired something of the dreaded utility man tag in his occasional first-team appearances. His goalscoring too was occasional, although he was tried at centre-forward on a couple of occasions later in the campaign as United's supply of goals from the more conventional strikers was in danger of drying up. The Sheffield United Cup-tie, however, where he was mobbed by delighted fans as he left the park, was probably his finest hour in a Carlisle jersey.

For the third time in a row Carlisle were drawn at home and this time against Arsenal. Beaten FA Cup finalists last season and double winners twelve months earlier, the Gunners were a formidable outfit who were top of the League when they travelled to Brunton Park on 24 February 1973. The draw was the trigger for a nostalgic look back to the famous 1951 tie where Carlisle had held the Cup holders to a goalless draw at Highbury. This time Carlisle had the advantage of being at home and a capacity crowd squeezed into Brunton Park for the big game, which also featured on *Match of the Day*. The Arsenal side that had completed the historic double in 1971 was still largely intact, though a notable addition was Alan Ball who had joined from Everton the previous year. Ball it was who gave Arsenal the lead after just six minutes before Dennis Martin's header brought the scores level just before half-time. Despite the urging of the majority of the 24,000 gate, it was the Arsenal captain Frank McLintock who broke the deadlock midway through the second half to clinch a 2-1 victory for the visitors. Although defeated, Carlisle had been far from disgraced in the company of one of the country's outstanding teams.

Now that Carlisle were out of the Cup, it was, in the words of the old cliché, time to concentrate on the League. Indeed it was evident from results in the early part of 1973 that United's concentration in this area had been somewhat lacking. Apart from in the FA Cup, Carlisle did not record a victory from Boxing Day 1972, when the massacre of Preston took place, until mid-March 1973, when Orient were beaten 1-0 thanks to Joe Laidlaw's goal with virtually the last kick of the match. By this time United had fallen to seventeenth place and looked in danger of relegation, a scenario that was hardly in the script for Alan Ashman's return to the club.

The causes of this poor run of results were much debated. Having bagged twenty goals between them in the first half of the season, both Laidlaw and Owen were struggling to score at all. Other players, too, were showing a loss of form and even Chris Balderstone was substituted on more than one occasion. Luckily Allan Ross in goal and the defenders in front of him were still performing to their usual standard and few defeats were by more than a one-goal margin. One team that did win more easily was QPR who ran out 3-1 winners at Brunton Park with Stan Bowles predictably among the scorers. The Rangers were the outstanding team in the division with the exception of Burnley, who had been held to a 1-1 draw on their own visit to Carlisle two weeks previously. The crowd of 17,842 was easily the best of the campaign, cup-ties excluded. The forthcoming tie with Arsenal did nevertheless play its part as spectators were issued with a voucher that they could exchange for a ticket for the big game to be played the following Saturday.

The win against Orient was one of only two victories in the last nineteen games of the season. The other win, which came two weeks later, was more surprising as it entailed a 2-0 defeat of Luton Town. This gave Carlisle their only double of the season, aided by a freak first goal when the Hatters' keeper palmed a harmless-looking cross from John Gorman into his own net. This result came just four days after United had travelled to visit Roker Park and a Sunderland side in the grip of FA Cup fever. On the night, Sunderland carried out their own voucher exercise to give supporters a chance to enter a ballot for Cup semi-final tickets against Arsenal. As a consequence, the crowd was 39,930, which at the time was the biggest gate ever to attend a League match involving Carlisle, beating the attendance of 36,842 who saw Hull City play the Cumbrians in the Third Division (North) in March 1949.

By the end of the campaign, Carlisle United had done just enough to stay in the division. Due to the poor second-half performance, United finished on 34 points and in nineteenth place. Huddersfield were relegated with one point fewer, although Carlisle did have the better goal-average, thanks to those home wins over Preston and Brighton by an aggregate of 11-2.

The curtain came down on the season with a home game against Aston Villa. Brian Tiler was made captain for the day against his old club and it was no surprise in such circumstances that he also scored his first goal for Carlisle. The match ended in a 2-2 draw, a result that left Aston Villa ending the season in third place, albeit eleven points behind QPR who in turn were one point adrift of champions Burnley. Twelve months later Carlisle would again end their season with a home match against Aston Villa but on this occasion it would not be the Villa who would be knocking on the door of the First Division.

CHAPTER 3

1973-74: Moving Up

Despite the draw against third-placed Aston Villa in the last match of the campaign, there was no doubt that the second half of the 1972-73 season was a severe disappointment for Carlisle United's players and supporters. While that match brought down the curtain on the Cumbrians' campaign, for one Second Division side at least there was still a job of work to be done. When Bob Stokoe arrived to take over at Sunderland's Roker Park in November of the previous year, the team was lying fifth from bottom of the Second Division, having won none of the last seven games and with crowds at home games down to barely 11,000. In fact, having spent the bulk of his playing career up the road at Newcastle's St James' Park, where he had won an FA Cup medal in 1955, his appointment as Sunderland boss was not even initially welcomed by many of the team's supporters.

Carlisle fans were as aware as anyone of the motivating powers of Bob Stokoe. Faced with an even more desperate situation when he arrived at Brunton Park in the autumn of 1968, he turned a team that already looked relegation certainties into fringe challengers for promotion using the same squad of players that he had inherited. At Sunderland he performed a similar feat. From lows of just over 11,000 the crowds at Roker Park gradually rose to over 40,000 for the final League game of the season, against QPR. The wonder of it was that once again he was working the transformation with players who were already at the club when he arrived. In early April, Sunderland defeated Arsenal, winners at Brunton Park just a few weeks earlier, in the Cup semi-final by a 2-1 margin to reach the FA Cup final. Their opponents at Wembley on 5 May 1973 were Leeds United. It was a day that no fan of the Black Cats will ever forget.

Among the many messages of good luck sent to Sunderland that week was one from the directors and players of Carlisle United. Bob Stokoe remained a popular figure at Brunton Park. Apart from his feat in turning round the club's fortunes in 1968, he had led the Cumbrians to the League Cup semi-final twelve months later, which they lost to Alan Ashman's West Bromwich Albion. At the time, it seemed as though the club would never again have a chance of playing at Wembley Stadium. This of course was long before the revival of the play-offs in 1987, an idea that had seemed to have fallen out of fashion at the end of the nineteenth century, not to mention the Associate Members Cup which dates from the 1983-84 season, although it has its origins in the Third Division Cup of the 1930s.

There is no doubt, moreover, that the presence of Sunderland in the Second Division was good news for Carlisle United. Even though the fortunes of the Roker men were at their lowest ebb when they came to Brunton Park in mid-November 1972, the crowd of nearly 9,000 was still among the season's best at Brunton Park. Four months later the gate for the return fixture at Roker was, as we have seen, almost 40,000. At that time, clubs did not keep all of their home gates but instead had to pay a portion to the visiting club, so that the share of a crowd over five times the usual home attendance would have provided a welcome boost to the Cumbrians' coffers. Carlisle's own home attendances in 1972-73 averaged a mere 7,606 which were, with the sole exception of Orient, the smallest in the Second Division.

As all the world knows, Sunderland defeated the Cup holders and hot favourites Leeds United 1-0 on that spring afternoon. Although the Black Cats had climbed the Second Division table during the Cup run, they were never genuine promotion candidates. The victory was, though, undoubtedly a boost for Second Division football and ensured that the fate of Sunderland in the following season might be of more than passing interest to followers of the game in general. Nor were the Roker club the only Second Division side attracting a level of media interest in the close season. The Charlton brothers both decided to hang up their boots and to enter management. Bobby Charlton played his final League game at Chelsea at the end of April, while elder brother Jack was making his own farewells at Leeds United. Days later it was announced that Jack Charlton would be the new boss at Middlesbrough. Bobby Charlton, meanwhile, was soon to find himself in the manager's chair at Preston's Deepdale ground.

The two sides relegated from the First Division were Crystal Palace and West Bromwich Albion. Palace had already completed the ascent from the Fourth Division to the First before dropping back to Division Two but in Malcolm Allison they possessed a manager who would have no difficulty keeping the club in the headlines, no matter how well or badly his team were to perform. West Bromwich Albion had a much more impressive pedigree in the top flight and the coming campaign would see them exiled from Division One for the first time since 1949. Don Howe, the man who had replaced Alan Ashman at the club two years earlier, was still at the helm, though relegation was surely far from the thoughts of the Albion directors when they had appointed Arsenal's double-winning coach as their manager.

The biggest club in the Second Division, Sunderland's Cup triumph notwithstanding, was however Aston Villa. Their average attendance in the season just gone was over 27,000, although that was actually 4,000 down on the previous season. In that year they had won the Division Three title to end their two-year sojourn outside the League's top two divisions and the momentum had carried them through to third place in the term just ended. Other members of the Second Division in that era included Portsmouth, Sheffield Wednesday, Bristol City and Nottingham Forest, all clubs whose football history and tradition were undeniably greater than that of Carlisle United.

History and tradition do not, however, guarantee success on the park and Alan Ashman was fully cognisant of the fact that his club would need to punch above its weight if it was to survive in Division Two. 'Not many people have mentioned Carlisle in next season's top ten' he mused at one point during the summer but 'we must get into the top ten' he continued.

Meanwhile, the Football League's annual general meeting, held on 1 June, was to take a decision that would alter Carlisle's history. The clubs voted to introduce a system of three up and three down between the First and Second Divisions and also between the Second and Third Divisions. Four up and four down would remain between the Third and Fourth. Ironically, Ashman himself was lukewarm about the idea, at least as far as the First/Second Divisions were concerned. He thought they should remain two up, two down. Presumably he was to change his mind by the end of the coming season, though at the time most people would have considered it far more likely the Cumbrians would finish third from bottom of the table than third from top.

Not that Alan Ashman would waste much time in looking to strengthen the squad once the campaign had ended. Within a week, two new faces had been recruited to Brunton Park. Mike McCartney was a player who could operate in a variety of positions and had just been released by West Brom. Still only eighteen, he had been a Scottish Schoolboy international before Ashman had brought him to the Hawthorns. The following week Carlisle bought Mick Barry from Huddersfield Town for a near club record £35,000. Mick celebrated his twentieth birthday just a few days after signing for Carlisle but had already played in the First Division for the Terriers. He had featured strongly in the Huddersfield Town team that had met United in the third round, where he had impressed with his passing and creative skills in midfield.

It was difficult not to view Barry as a possible long-term replacement for Chris Balderstone, not least because like Balderstone he had come from Huddersfield Town. Indeed it seemed for a time that Carlisle might be needing to replace Chris Balderstone rather more quickly than many would have anticipated.

All through his career, Chris Balderstone had been torn between the competing demands of football and cricket. There was a time when the two sports could happily coexist. The football season ended in the last week of April and did not begin again until the start of September. That left four months of fairly uninterrupted time for cricket, the presumption being that players kept fit for one game by playing the other. Double football and cricket internationals were far from unknown, although the last one, Arthur Milton of Arsenal and Gloucestershire, earned his international honours in the 1950s. Chris Balderstone was, as we have seen, inspired by Willie Watson, another double international who had attended the same school in Huddersfield.

Gradually the football season extended into May at one end and August at the other, and it became harder and harder to successfully combine careers in both sports. Chris himself actually played relatively little first-class cricket in his ten years at Yorkshire, most of his appearances coming when more senior players were called away on Test match duty. It was not until 1967 that his career total of first-class runs even reached one thousand, and in his last year with the White Rose county, his games in the first team were confined to two John Player Sunday matches. That, though, was to change in 1971 when he joined Leicestershire by special registration. The captain at Grace Road was Ray Illingworth, another Yorkshire exile, as was Jack Burkinshaw, while Graham Cross of Leicester City was another footballer/cricketer at the club.

Chris Balderstone played ten County Championship games that season. The following year, his cricketing days were restricted by Carlisle's participation in the Anglo-Italian Tournament. In his brief time at Grace Road, however, he helped Leicestershire to win the Benson & Hedges Trophy, being named Man of the Match in the final against Yorkshire at Lords.

In 1973 Balderstone's cricket continued to progress. He scored his maiden first-class century against Lancashire and shortly afterwards was awarded his county cap. By the end of the cricket season he had passed 1,000 runs for the first time, as well as taking twenty wickets with his slow left-arm spin. He was even being talked about as a possible selection for England's forthcoming winter tour to the West Indies. Unfortunately, this progress was achieved at the expense of his football commitments. He was club captain at Brunton Park and had already signed a new contract for the forthcoming season. One of the clauses stated that he would be available to return to Carlisle for training in July.

Carlisle United were not unaware of this conflict of loyalties and he was granted a week's grace before he had to return. Leicestershire were involved in a Gillette Cup quarter-final on 1 August and Chris was instructed to report to Brunton Park the following day. Leicestershire lost their cup-tie to Worcestershire, but the following day found Chris not at Carlisle but still in Leicester preparing for a county championship game. He was immediately suspended by United and stripped of the captaincy.

The Balderstone affair was not Alan Ashman's only problem in the close season. The successful recruitment of Mick Barry and Mike McCartney had been followed by a period of frustration as the manager failed to add a much-needed striker to the squad. The signing of Kenny Wilson had clearly been an expensive mistake and he was the principal casualty when the retained list was announced, being put on the transfer list for £15,000. The club then made great efforts to replace him, targeting first Peter Noble of relegated Swindon Town and then Billy Rafferty who was at Blackpool. Noble decided to join Burnley, newly promoted to Division One, where he went on to have a very successful career. The much-travelled Rafferty stayed at Blackpool until 1974 when he moved to Plymouth, where he formed a successful partnership with Paul Mariner. Eventually, of course, Carlisle United did manage to secure his signature, but not until 1976. Hugh McIlmoyle, who had been released by Preston, was also targeted by United but again no agreement could be reached. The club had a relatively flat wage structure which had its advantages but also its drawbacks when it came to signing new players. Geography too could play a part, though since Rafferty and McIlmoyle were Scots and Noble hailed from the North East, this should not have been a major factor in these cases.

The start of July did, however, see one very significant addition to the United squad. Bill Green was only 22 but was already the captain at Fourth Division Hartlepool, for whom he had played well over a century of League matches. The cost of his signature was £15,000 but it would prove to be money well spent. Intelligent and a natural leader, his rise to the captaincy at Brunton Park would be much swifter than he could have expected when he joined the Cumbrians.

The search for a striker continued and it was only a week before the season began that Frank Clarke joined Carlisle United. The eldest of five brothers who all played League football, Frank was 31 when he signed and a veteran of over 300 games for Shrewsbury, QPR, and most recently Bobby Robson's Ipswich. A proven goalscorer at all his former clubs, he was an experienced and unselfish player who was adept at holding the ball and combining with his fellow forwards.

The club began its short programme of pre-season friendlies at Berwick Rangers of the Scottish Second Division. In the absence of the suspended Balderstone, Stan Ternent took over the captaincy as United won 1-0 at Shielfield Park. This match also saw the first outing for the club's new strip of blue shirts with a white facing edged with red on each side. Thirty years on it remains one of the club's most distinctive strips, not least through being associated with the Division One campaign. The win at Berwick was followed by another at Oldham, with Kenny Wilson scoring a rare goal to add to that of Bobby Owen. Ex-United winger George McVitie was in the Oldham team. Four days later the last friendly match was played at Workington. The Reds won 2-0 but the game was marred by outbreaks of hooliganism and 34 arrests among the 2,250 crowd. It was hardly the ideal curtain-raiser to the new campaign.

The Football League season finally began in earnest on 25 August 1973 when Cardiff made the long trek north. The ground itself had seen one major change during the summer months as a proper perimeter wall had been constructed around the terraces, replacing the wooden paling fence that had been in place for many years. As for the Carlisle team that kicked off the new campaign, Bill Green and Frank Clarke both lined up to make their debuts but there was no place for either the suspended Balderstone or, more surprisingly, Mick Barry. The Bluebirds had actually finished below Carlisle in the season just ended, avoiding relegation only on goal-average. It was no surprise therefore when Frank Clarke put United ahead after only nine minutes. Sadly, Carlisle could not put the game beyond the visitors' reach and five minutes from the end a penalty from Gary Bell, Cardiff's spot-kick specialist, made the scores level.

Three days later Workington made the short journey to Brunton Park for a first round League Cup-tie. It was United's first appearance for nine years in the opening stage of the competition and the visit of a struggling Fourth Division outfit must have seemed a fairly kind draw. The Reds, though, had won 2-0 at Carlisle when the two clubs had met on a previous occasion in the same competition and at half-time they held a 2-0 lead, despite the absence through suspension of Johnny Martin their star forward. It was left to Frank Clarke to again prove his worth as he twice set up Bobby Owen, whose second-half goals ensured a replay at Borough Park a week later. This time an early Les O'Neill goal meant that Carlisle went through, while just as importantly the Cumbria Constabulary were relieved that the incidents experienced in the 'friendly' match were not replicated in real competition.

Interspersed between the two games with Workington, United travelled to Luton Town for their first away match. Kenilworth Road had been the scene of United's only away win in the season just gone. Moreover no Carlisle side had ever before lost to Luton. No record lasts for ever, but few can have been lost so emphatically as Carlisle conceded six goals in a twenty-minute spell in the first half. The report that the defence 'lacked method, understanding and determination' was something of an understatement. Bob Delgado, whose own career had begun at Kenilworth Road, came off the bench for the injured Ray Train and his more vigorous approach at least kept the deficit at six, while Bobby Owen pulled back a consolation goal in the second half to make the final score 6-1.

Chris Balderstone had been training since returning north in mid-August but he had been forced to train alone as his suspension was renewed not just once but twice, and it was well into September before the suspension was lifted and he was allowed to train with the rest of the squad. Carlisle could, in fact, have sold him in this period as Bob Stokoe, a long-time admirer of his talent, made a £15,000 bid to take him across to Roker Park. At the time, Sunderland must have seemed to Chris a far better bet for promotion to the First Division and the chance of performing in the top flight but the United directors would not hear of it. A transfer request from Bob Delgado was also turned down at the same time, although the luckless Kenny Wilson was allowed to go to York City on trial with a view to a permanent move. Although he scored for York's reserve team, the two first-team games in which he would feature both ended as goalless draws.

On 18 September, Chris Balderstone finally returned to the United line up. The crowd gave him a warm reception but two second-half goals handed Pompey both points. The defeat pushed Carlisle down to second from bottom, as well as earning the visitors their first win of the season. Stan Ternent was dropped and Bill Green, who had already stood in as captain in the game at Borough Park, was given the captain's armband on a more permanent basis. It was arguably the turning point of the season as United began to climb the table. Four days later, an Oxford United side that featured Derek Clarke, one of Frank's younger brothers, was defeated 2-1 at Brunton Park. Frank himself opened the scoring in what was only Carlisle's second League win of the term.

There were celebrations of a different kind off the pitch as United's veteran mascot 'Twinkletoes', or George Baxter to give him his proper name, was presented with a gift of beer cans to mark his 1,000th appearance as the club's mascot. Dressed in his blue hat and tails and white trousers, his pre-match hop and skip onto the pitch carrying 'Olga' the stuffed fox had been an integral feature of any visit to Brunton Park for more than twenty years, while for the former drayman at the Carlisle Brewery, his celebratory gift was nothing if not appropriate. Such was his dedication, I was once told, that he did not take any annual holidays but instead took 21 Saturday mornings off to ensure he did not miss a United away match.

A week after defeating Oxford, United made the traditionally difficult trip to Millwall. Arguably, the Den was the most intimidating venue in the Football League at the time and in twelve previous visits not only had Carlisle never claimed both points but only twice had they even managed a draw. When Gordon Bolland's twenty-yard shot skidded past Allan Ross in the Carlisle goal just ten minutes from the end, it looked as though the thirteenth visit would be as proverbially unlucky as the rest. Within a minute, the Lions' centre-half Barry Kitchener, in attempting to clear a harmless cross, headed into his own net as his goalkeeper advanced into no-man's-land between the goal-line and his defence. As full-time approached, Carlisle won a free-kick deep inside the Millwall half and Mick Barry's well-flighted kick was headed into the net by Bill Green.

Watching this drama on the crumbling terraces of the Den, I thought it safest to keep my delight to myself. The reaction of at least one member of the Millwall team has however also been recorded for posterity. Eamonn Dunphy wore the No 10 shirt that day for the Lions. He later wrote a book *Only a Game?* which covered the first half of Millwall's 1973-74 season. Regarded as a minor classic, his verdict on his team's performance against Carlisle is as direct and to the point as might be expected of the subsequent biographer of Roy Keane.

Gradually Carlisle's crowd figures began to improve, along with the results at Brunton Park. The gate of only 5,093 that saw the victory over Oxford was the club's lowest ever Second Division crowd. Over 8,300 witnessed the next home game that saw Bolton Wanderers defeated, despite Mick Barry's dismissal for retaliation in the first half. Two weeks later the attendance for the visit of leaders Middlesbrough exceeded 11,000 as the two sides played out a 1-1 draw. This time it was the visitors who were down to ten men when Graeme Souness was dismissed following an off-the-ball incident involving Stan Ternent. Souness apparently later described Ternent as the hardest tackler he ever faced, a judgment that may give a clue to the reason for his early bath.

When United overcame Fulham four days later, it brought their haul to eight points from the last ten and had moved them up to seventh in the table. One of the Carlisle goals resulted from a fumble by Peter Mellor in the Fulham goal. Unfortunately for the Cumbrians, Mellor's next appearance at Brunton Park was to be rather more polished, as we shall see later on. One of the surprising features of this run of form was that it took place without both Mick Barry and Chris Balderstone, regarded as the obvious playmakers of the squad. Barry was suspended for three games after his dismissal against Bolton, while Balderstone had suffered a broken nose in the League Cup-tie at Gillingham which United won 2-1, a result that earned Carlisle a home draw against First Division Manchester City. Some of Carlisle's more unsettled players meanwhile were being farmed out to other clubs, which kept them fit and also reduced the wage roll at the club. Kenny Wilson and Bob Delgado were loaned to Workington, while Steve Derrett made the much longer journey south to Third Division Aldershot.

By the end of October the eventual League table usually begins to take shape. The teams at the top are generally there or thereabouts at the end and the same goes for those near the bottom. Middlesbrough were clearly the division's pace-setters with eight wins and only one defeat in their fourteen games, despite averaging only a goal a game. Aston Villa too had made a good start to the season and were lying second, three points behind. More surprisingly, Orient were lying third, having, like Carlisle, improved from an indifferent start to the campaign.

Conversely, some of the more fancied outfits were finding life in the Second Division more of a struggle. Sunderland, following their FA Cup triumph, were naturally among the favourites for promotion but they were finding the burden of expectation rather too great despite attracting the largest crowds. Among the newly relegated teams, West Bromwich Albion were no more than mid-table, though like everyone else they were looking down on Crystal Palace. The Glaziers were still seeking their first win of the term, yet an average crowd of over 19,000 was a testament to the strength of their support. At this stage it was the third highest in the division and contrasted with Carlisle's average of barely 7,300, which at that time was the lowest in Division Two.

United's next home fixture attracted the best gate of the season to date but it was for the League Cup encounter against First Division Manchester City. Three years earlier, the two clubs had met in the same competition and Carlisle had come through before a crowd of almost 18,000. This time the attendance was a more modest 14,472, even though this game was played at a later stage of the competition. No fewer than eight of the City side from three years earlier returned to Brunton Park, while Carlisle boasted a further four survivors. At times the visitors rode their luck, not least when Carlisle hit the woodwork twice in a minute in the second half. United also suffered injuries to both central defenders in

Bill Green and Brian Tiler. Clearly the fates had decided that there was to be no repeat of the result of three years earlier and this was confirmed by Francis Lee's breakaway strike late in the second half, shortly after the Manchester City post had demonstrated its charmed life. City eventually went on to reach the final before losing 1-2 to Wolves.

Although disappointing, defeat by Manchester City did not adversely affect United's form in the League and a 4-0 victory over Hull the following weekend pushed Carlisle up to sixth place and what would prove to be the club's highest position of the calendar year. A week later, the seven-match unbeaten streak ended at Nottingham Forest as the run up to Christmas produced a mixed bag of results. The home defeat by Blackpool was in a sense no surprise as the Seasiders had often proved to be one of Carlisle's bogey teams. The 2-3 reverse was the fourth occasion in six visits that Blackpool had gone away with both points. Messrs Green and Tiler both returned to the side after injury, and hence Les O'Neill gave up his role as stand-in captain.

O'Neill had thrived on the responsibility with some outstanding displays as a ball-winner in midfield. He was also the scorer of goals against both Bristol City and Blackpool. The latter effort, a full-length header while lying prone after his shot had hit the post, was his fifth of the season, an outstanding return for a supposedly defensive midfielder. Two weeks later, a family bereavement kept him out of the home game against Millwall and it was perhaps no accident that Carlisle only managed a 1-1 draw in a lacklustre display. Eamonn Dunphy was not, however, in the visiting team that day and his opinion sadly is unrecorded.

Seven days earlier, United had redeemed themselves after losing to Blackpool by winning 1-0 at Orient. Although it was a second successive home defeat for the O's, it only pushed them down into third place, while the attendance of 7,645 proved to be almost the lowest of the season at Brisbane Road. Their average gate, in fact, was running at double the figure of the previous season, and they had in Bullock, Fairbrother and Queen three of the leading scorers in the division. Orient had been something of a revelation with their 'push and run' style of football and had dominated the game before Dennis Martin's snap shot nine minutes from the end produced the game's only goal.

Earlier in the second half, Mike McCartney had come off the bench to make his Football League debut. Until that day, his only football since arriving in the summer after his release from West Brom had been playing for the 'A' team in the Carlisle & District League. It would still be some time before he established himself in the United line up, though at the age of nineteen he was still much the youngest member of the

Carlisle squad. As it was, he was actually on the brink of a career that, as will be noted later on, would be remarkable for its longevity.

Just as Mike McCartney's career was beginning, so Messrs Delgado and Derrett were coming to the end of their days at Brunton Park. Bob Delgado had enjoyed a successful loan spell at Workington and the Reds had extended it for a second month. One of his games was at Rotherham and the upshot was that a few days later, the Millers secured his signature for a £7,000 fee. Very shortly afterwards Steve Derrett also followed him to South Yorkshire, where between them they would play over 200 games in the next three seasons. A further move also seemed to be on the cards as Hamilton Academical were reported to be interested in acquiring the services of Kenny Wilson, though as the year ended he was still based at Brunton Park.

The home match with Millwall just before Christmas brought Carlisle's season to its halfway mark. At this point, the Cumbrians were lying tenth but apart from Middlesbrough, who were seven points clear, the division was very tightly contested. Second-placed Luton Town, for example, who were due at Brunton Park on New Year's Day, were only four points ahead of Carlisle. With two of the next three games to be played against teams above them in the table, Carlisle fans had good reason to look forward to the forthcoming holiday period, not to mention the prospect of witnessing FA Cup holders Sunderland begin the defence of their trophy at Brunton Park in the first weekend of the New Year.

CHAPTER 4

1973-74: Perfect Timing

Boxing Day 1973 saw United make the comparatively short trip down the M6 to Deepdale and Preston North End. The Lilywhites had hit the headlines in the summer by appointing Bobby Charlton to his first managerial role after retiring as a player from Manchester United. At first, things had gone well for the new boss and, after defeating Sunderland in October, Preston had briefly reached third place in the table. Thereafter, things began to go downhill, despite the signing of Manchester United veterans Nobby Stiles and David Sadler, and by Christmas they were in the bottom half of the table. Carlisle, meanwhile, were becoming one of the division's form teams and won with the only goal of the game, even if Ray Train's 30-yard strike owed something to Healey's fumble in the Preston goal.

Three days later, Carlisle won again on their travels, this time at Notts County. The Magpies, too, were promotion contenders, although their confidence was no doubt shaken by their loss at local rivals Nottingham Forest on Boxing Day. They must have been even more shell-shocked when Carlisle raced into a two-goal lead after just four minutes, both efforts courtesy of Joe Laidlaw. Laidlaw had been an ever-present in the campaign but his haul of only three goals to date did not really reflect the contribution he made to the side with his powerful direct running at defences. His style was described by one local scribe around this time as 'about as subtle as a bulldozer in the Amazon rainforest', a comment that not only gives a flavour of Joe Laidlaw at his best but also shows that the problems of Amazon deforestation are at least 30 years old. Joe Laidlaw could have had a hat-trick against Notts County but Carlisle's third and final goal was another Laidlaw strike that was turned into his own net by Notts County defender David McVay.

It was Carlisle's third successive away win and the fifth in all so far in the season, a far cry from 1972-73 when only once did the club gain both points on their travels. The most immediate effect of this run of results was to earn for Alan Ashman the Second Division's Manager of the Month award for December. It was the first time he had won such an honour, which he modestly described as in reality belonging to Dick Young and to the players as well as to himself. It was nevertheless a fillip to the whole club, particularly in the light of the poor start that had been made to the season. As New Year's Day 1974 dawned, it no longer seemed fanciful to speculate on the chance of promotion to the First Division.

Such sentiments could only have been encouraged by the victory that same day against Luton Town. Luton had been a First Division side when they lost to Nottingham Forest in the 1959 Cup final but thereafter they had suffered a rapid decline. They were relegated to Division Four the same year Carlisle were Third Division champions but gradually they had clawed their way back up the leagues. They were now hoping to become the first club to drop from the First Division to the Fourth before rising all the way back to Division One. Financial problems had previously caused the Hatters to sell talented players such as Don Givens and Malcolm MacDonald. Manager Harry Haslam, however, had bought wisely, recruiting Alan West from Burnley, Jimmy Husband from Everton and Johnny Aston from Manchester United. On the day, however, United were unfazed and after a hard-fought first half scored twice after the interval through a Bill Green header and a clever Dennis Martin goal set up by Joe Laidlaw.

The victory raised Carlisle back up to fourth place but for now all First and Second Division sides could take a break from the League to concentrate on the FA Cup. For once, the third round draw had done Carlisle a huge favour, giving them a home tie against holders Sunderland. Soon after the draw was made, United announced that the crowd limit for the game would be 25,400. The game was made all-ticket but a scheme to distribute vouchers to the crowd attending the Millwall game just before Christmas failed to attract the anticipated surge in attendance. Sunderland were undeniably an attraction but not perhaps as big as might have been thought. It also became known that the *Match of the Day* cameras would not be allowed into the ground, due to the modest fee that was on offer from the BBC. Unlike today, when virtually all competitive games are routinely filmed and/or broadcast, the televising of any particular fixture was still at times a hit or miss affair. The decision not to allow the match to be shown was not popular with some of Carlisle's older fans but the club stuck to its guns.

In the event, the match at Brunton Park attracted a gate of just over 20,500 and it ended in a goalless draw. Sunderland included eight of their Cup-winning eleven and it was one of the eight who came closest to scoring when Vic Halom's 30-yard drive bounced back off the crossbar. Judging by the two sides' respective League performances, Sunderland had done well to earn the replay. On New Year's Day, they had lost 1-2 at home to Notts County, where United had won 3-0 three days earlier – a result that pushed Sunderland into the bottom half of the table. Four days after the draw at Brunton Park, Sunderland's grip on the FA Cup came to an end as they went down 0-1 in the replay at Roker Park. In another hard-fought encounter it was Dennis Martin who broke the deadlock with a twenty-yard snap-shot into the corner of the goal after the home side's defence was caught napping. It was a typical piece of quick thinking by the Carlisle forward. Something of a touch player who often seemed to lack confidence in his undoubted ability, it was the second time in under a month that his flash of inspiration had been the difference between Carlisle and their opponents.

Carlisle's reward for overcoming the FA Cup holders was the chance to play the League champions. Liverpool's seven years without a trophy had ended in 1973 when they clinched both the League title and the UEFA Cup. It was to be Bill Shankly's last season in charge at the club, although this only became public after the season had ended. On the face of it, United appeared to have little chance of even avoiding defeat at Anfield. The Reds were unbeaten at home all season, apart from losing in the European Cup to Red Star Belgrade. Moreover, they had won all but one of their home League games and had never failed to score. Yet in the previous round they had only drawn at home to Doncaster Rovers, who were bottom of the Fourth Division, before winning the replay.

Liverpool took no chances and in the stand for Carlisle's home match with Sheffield Wednesday was their chief scout Geoff Twentyman. He was more entitled than most to be sitting in the stand as he had indirectly helped the club to construct the building in 1954. The previous edifice, Shankly's 'glorified hencoop', had burned down in March 1953. Fundraising to build a replacement stand was slow in coming and it was only the sale of Carlisle's rising centre-half Geoff Twentyman to Liverpool for £12,500 in December 1953 that helped to turn the plans for a new stand into reality.

Both Twentyman and Shankly enjoyed returning to the club where they had begun their careers but they also knew who paid their wages and they were determined that Carlisle's interest in the Cup would soon come to an end. United, though, were undaunted as manager Alan Ashman ruled out any special preparations before the tie, preferring to adopt the club's usual routine during the week before travelling to Merseyside on the Friday. Carlisle fans were, however, more excited by the prospect and some 7,000 made their way down to Liverpool.

What they witnessed was a remarkable performance by Carlisle who held the Reds to a goalless draw before over 47,000 fans. To say that Allan Ross was the busier of the two goalkeepers would be no exaggeration as Liverpool completely dominated the match without being able to score.

Particularly impressive was Chris Balderstone who had found a new role for the club as sweeper. Never the fastest player on the pitch, even in his younger days, he more than compensated for this with his speed of thought. 'He runs the first two yards in his head' was a popular verdict on his abilities. His calm and authoritative play belied the fact that it was only against Sunderland that he had even adopted the role when he came off the bench to replace the injured Brian Tiler. It was one he would largely retain for the rest of the season.

The replay three days later took place on the Tuesday afternoon. Britain had been in the grip of a political and industrial crisis since before Christmas. Faced with the problems of union militancy at home, compounded by a quadrupling of the oil price following the Yom Kippur war, the Government of Edward Heath had declared a three-day working week with the use of floodlights banned to save energy.

The Sunderland replay had been played on a Wednesday afternoon and this time a crowd of over 21,000 wended its way to Brunton Park to see if the team lying second in Division One would suffer Sunderland's fate.

It was not to be, but Carlisle went out of the competition beaten but not disgraced. The first half was again goalless but this time two second-half goals enabled the Merseysiders to progress to the fifth round. Financially, Carlisle had enjoyed a highly successful Cup run as the four matches attracted a total of almost 115,000 spectators, the game at Anfield alone earning net receipts of over £7,000. Liverpool went on to win that year's FA Cup, defeating a disappointing Newcastle United in the final. Carlisle meanwhile had plenty of reasons of their own to give their undivided attention to the Second Division promotion race.

The run of form that had propelled the club to fourth place in the table and a Manager of the Month award was less in evidence for a while as cup-ties appeared to take precedence. Sheffield Wednesday took a two-goal lead at Brunton Park before Carlisle equalised, the second goal from Bobby Owen coming in the last minute of the game. In the next match it was Frank Clarke who grabbed a late equaliser at Cardiff in a match played in the morning to allow Welsh fans to watch the Wales versus Scotland rugby match in the afternoon.

Two weeks later it was Orient who made the long trip north to face not just Carlisle but the *Match of the Day* cameras who were now allowed into Brunton Park. Though both sides had played Cup replays in mid-week, the match proved to be one of the most entertaining seen at Brunton Park all season. For once, Carlisle were probably flattered by the 3-0 scoreline, with Frank Clarke netting twice. Yet for many the abiding memory was of goalkeeper Allan Ross coolly dribbling past an Orient forward before clearing the ball, an episode that also featured in the programme's closing credits.

With hindsight, that victory over Orient was one of the most crucial of the season. It meant that Carlisle had now completed the double over one of their closest rivals and ultimately it was United who would deprive the Londoners of that third promotion place a few weeks later. Despite their defeat, Orient remained second while Carlisle stayed two slots below them. The defeat, however, heralded a surprising drop in the form of the London club. They would win just two of their remaining fifteen League fixtures and with that record, the wonder is that they were still promotion contenders until the very end of the campaign.

For Carlisle, that victory was the club's last League game for three weeks. The following Saturday, Carlisle were due to travel to play Oxford at the Manor Ground. Heavy rain had fallen in the Oxford area but it appeared to have cleared and the game rather frustratingly was not called off until very late in the day. The following Saturday was the FA Cup fifth round. Although Carlisle were now eliminated, their intended opponents West Bromwich Albion were still in the Cup, though not for much longer after they lost 0-3 to Newcastle. To avoid a second successive weekend of inactivity, Carlisle organised a trip to York's Bootham Crescent to play a friendly match against one of the Third Division's strongest sides. York, in fact, would become the first in their own division to clinch promotion through finishing in third place and they proved to be too strong for Carlisle, winning 2-1.

One player who did not travel to York was Kenny Wilson. Hamilton Academical's interest in him before Christmas seemed to have cooled but after negotiations were revived, he joined the Scottish club on a free transfer and made his debut for the Accies on the day of the York City game. So ended one of the most disappointing of all Carlisle transfer sagas. Wilson was essentially a goal-poacher and being charitable, his style of play seldom seemed to gel with the rest of the team while the loss on the deal of £36,000 speaks for itself.

Finally, United returned to League action on the last Saturday of the month with a visit to Bolton Wanderers. The Trotters were another club who had under-achieved in much of the campaign but they were unbeaten in seven games when they entertained Carlisle on 23 February. Playing in the Bolton line up was Peter Thompson, the ex-Harraby School pupil who had played for England Schoolboys before joining Preston and later Liverpool. While at Anfield, he had also earned sixteen England caps to become the first Carlisle-born player to represent his country. Now in the twilight of his career, he had recently signed for the Burnden Park outfit that would prove to be his last club.

Peter Thompson was never on the books at Brunton Park but one who did hold that distinction was Bolton's full-back Peter Nicholson. Born in Cleator Moor, he would spend the bulk of his footballing days at Burnden Park, though he was briefly to appear for Carlisle some years later. Bolton extended their unbeaten run to eight matches with a 2-0 victory over Carlisle and two days later West Brom took both points in their first ever League visit to Brunton Park. With the three-day week and floodlight ban still in operation, the game was played on the Monday afternoon. It was a scrappy affair, being decided by a single goal for the Baggies following a rare defensive error by Chris Balderstone. The result enabled the visitors to climb above United as Carlisle dropped down to sixth following this second successive defeat.

To many it must have appeared that these two consecutive reverses would have all but ended Carlisle's promotion chances. There was certainly no real prospect of ending the term as champions. Middlesbrough under Jack Charlton had topped the table since September and were currently seven points clear of second-placed Luton. The Hatters in turn were two points in front of Orient but thereafter Blackpool, West Brom and Nottingham Forest, as well as Carlisle, were all in with a shout. Nor could clubs such as Sunderland be discounted as they had games in hand on most of the teams above them. At the risk of stating the obvious, the decision to promote three teams had certainly opened up the promotion prospects for a number of sides.

Not that United did much in their next match to enhance their promotion push. Facing lowly Preston at home, Carlisle were two goals down at half-time, both efforts courtesy of Preston's debutant Mike Elwiss. Elwiss would turn out to be a good signing for Preston but he was playing in a struggling side. In the second half United equalised and by the end the Lilywhites were hanging on to earn a point. Both sides really needed a victory, though for Preston, who were to win only one of their last thirteen games, the need was arguably the greater. At least Carlisle were not in danger of relegation.

Off the field the news was mixed for Carlisle's squad. Brian Tiler, back in the side against Preston, asked for a transfer as he was not getting regular first-team football. It was a perpetual problem for a one-team club such as Carlisle to satisfy everyone. Tot Winstanley and Stan Ternent were other capable defenders who had earlier requested moves for similar reasons. Mick Barry too had made only sporadic first-team appearances but in his case it was injury that was keeping him on the sidelines.

It was now confirmed that he would be out for the rest of the campaign. On a happier note, John Gorman was voted into the Second Division Select, at what were the first annual PFA awards, as recognition of his excellent performances. Twice previously Player of the Season at Brunton Park, he would be many people's choice to make it three in a row. Carlisle could also bask in the reflected glory of locally born Kevin Beattie being chosen as the first ever Young Player of the Year due to his performances for Ipswich Town. A further cause for celebration was the call up of Stan Bowles into the England squad.

Carlisle, though, were needing to get back into the winning habit and did so in the next match away at Fulham's Craven Cottage, where they dominated proceedings to win 2-0. It also confirmed London somewhat improbably as a new favourite destination for the club. United' success at the Cottage completed a quartet of victories at all four London venues of Orient, Fulham, Millwall and Crystal Palace. Furthermore, only Millwall, who managed a draw before Christmas, were to escape defeat on their journeys north to Brunton Park.

Since I was based in London at the time, this is one aspect of the promotion campaign that I can recall with especial enjoyment. A week after the win at Fulham, Carlisle duly completed their London club fixtures with a laboured victory over Crystal Palace at Brunton Park. Palace had been having a wretched season with only two wins in the first half of the campaign. Since Christmas their form had improved considerably and they had climbed off the bottom of the division but without looking as though they would reach safety. Carlisle's victory was therefore no real surprise but the narrowness of the margin meant the result was always in doubt. The catalogue of missed chances also meant that an opportunity to improve the side's goal-average was also lost.

For once, that chance was taken a couple of weeks later when Swindon Town were the visitors to Brunton Park. The Robins had won only one of their last eighteen matches and had been anchored at the foot of the table since early February when they had been overtaken by a resurgent Crystal Palace. The United eleven was unchanged from that which had drawn at Hull the previous weekend, which meant that Frank Clarke would be in the line up against Swindon.

It had been a difficult few months for Clarke as his family were still based three hundred miles away down in Ipswich until he sold his house. It was hardly an ideal commuting distance and he had been reluctant to move into a club house, even on a temporary basis, in case it disrupted his daughter's schooling. Such was his dilemma at one point that he had even asked for a transfer. Finally the house in Ipswich was sold and in mid-March the family were able to move up to Carlisle on a permanent basis.

It was as if a weight had been lifted from his shoulders and it was the men from Wiltshire who were to suffer the consequences. At the County Ground it was Frank Clarke who had scored both Carlisle goals in the opening ten minutes of the match. After eleven minutes of the return fixture history had repeated itself as he had again twice hit the target. This time he went not one but two goals better, becoming the first United player since Bob Hatton in December 1970 to score four goals in a game. His third goal was a penalty, a fact notable not just because it completed the hat-trick but it was also the first spot-kick Carlisle had been awarded all season. Joe Laidlaw too weighed in with a brave diving header to score Carlisle's third goal of the game. Despite Swindon scoring a late consolation effort, the overall 5-1 result was one of the most satisfying of the season. It was Carlisle's biggest win and also Swindon's heaviest defeat and the only disappointment from the home side's point of view was the modest gate of 6,544. It was possible that a few fans had decided to stay at home to watch the Grand National. Even in this respect it was Frank Clarke's day as he had picked out Red Rum in the club sweepstake.

The win over Swindon pushed Carlisle back up to fourth, level on points with Blackpool (third) and Orient (fifth). Luton were two points ahead while Middlesbrough were already promoted and champions in all but name. Boro had lost just twice all season and were currently in a run of nine consecutive victories. Unsurprisingly, they possessed the meanest defence in the division, with the very names of such as Craggs, Boam, Maddren and Spraggon conveying an air of resistance and solidity in front of goalkeeper Platt. In midfield they had the redoubtable Graeme Souness and Bobby Murdoch, the ex-Celtic player who had been one of the Lisbon Lions. Murdoch was a fine passer of the ball and he and David Armstrong would feed not just the front pair of Mills and Hickton but also Alan Foggon who would break quickly from midfield. As a tactical plan it was brilliant and Foggon's nineteen goals made him the club's top scorer.

Middlesbrough had also been consistent, unlike all their rivals who had dropped points throughout the campaign. In fact, as far as United were concerned, Ashman was eventually authorised by the directors to state that the club definitely wanted promotion. It was an attempt to scotch the theory that Carlisle would rather be a fairly good Second Division side than take their chance of promotion to the top flight.

That theory was soon put to the test as Carlisle duly lost their next two games. Bristol City is another of those grounds where the Cumbrians have tasted success all too rarely. Mike McCartney came in for his full debut that day in place of the injured Les O'Neill and in a match refereed by Jack Taylor – who three months later would be taking charge of the World Cup final in Munich – Bristol were comfortable 2-0 winners. Six days later Carlisle travelled to Sunderland on Good Friday at the start of the three-match Easter programme. The Black Cats had been gradually moving back up the table with a run of seven wins in ten games and naturally wanted revenge for their Cup defeat by Carlisle. It was United who took the lead early in the second half through Joe Laidlaw but, for the only time all season, Carlisle were to lose a game where they had been in front. Sunderland's 2-1 win thus pushed them briefly back above United in the table.

The next day Bob Stokoe's men were brought back to earth, losing at home to Bristol City. Carlisle meanwhile welcomed Nottingham Forest, a club they had never previously beaten in the League and who were just below them in the table. The Forest star was Duncan McKenzie who by now had emerged as the Second Division's top goalscorer. Bright and very much an individual, given to vaulting over Mini cars and similar stunts, his form had earned him a place in the England squad although he never did win a full cap for his country. It was he who put Forest ahead with a typical piece of individual skill just before half-time. After the interval it was Bobby Owen, in for the injured Frank Clarke, who equalised with a brilliant header, having typically missed a much easier chance. Both points were then clinched by a fine solo effort from Joe Laidlaw that hauled the Carlisle promotion bid back on track.

At last the Carlisle public was beginning to sense it could be United's year. The gate had been over 9,000 for the visit of Forest and a gate of some 14,000 was confidently expected for the visit of Sunderland on Easter Tuesday. For once, the newspaper estimate was too cautious as a total of 19,692 fans, then Carlisle's second largest League crowd ever, made their way to Brunton Park on that fine spring evening. Even allowing for an away contingent of over 2,000, the home support must have been in the order of 17,000. It was the fourth meeting that season between the two sides and again there was little to choose between them – they knew each other so well. In the end, luck was the vital ingredient and it was Carlisle who received the vital breaks. In the first half Longhorn came closest to scoring when his fierce drive crashed against the Carlisle woodwork with Allan Ross well beaten. The decisive point in the match came early in the second half when Joe Laidlaw, having beaten two defenders on a typical surging run, was brought down on the edge of the Sunderland penalty area. The referee ruled it was inside and Chris

Balderstone smashed the resulting spot-kick past Jimmy Montgomery for the game's only goal.

That victory virtually ended Sunderland's promotion hopes but Carlisle were still in the hunt for third place, especially as they were due at Blackpool four days later. It was an unchanged team who travelled to Bloomfield Road accompanied by a large travelling support. This time it was Carlisle who twice – through Owen and Laidlaw – hit the woodwork and it was the Seasiders who scored four times to put themselves in the driving seat for that third promotion spot, two points ahead of United and with a much superior goal-average. The Cumbrians, on the other hand, were now facing the final two games without captain Bill Green whose total of bookings had earned him a two-match ban.

The Oxford United game should have been played in February but Alan Ashman now took virtually the full squad down to the City of Dreaming Spires (though the alternative title of City of Lost Causes would hopefully not be appropriate), including the suspended Bill Green. Even a little sightseeing was arranged to lessen any anxiety about the forthcoming vital match, an initiative which smacks of a typical piece of Ashman psychology.

The League table was such that Carlisle needed a win to retain any realistic chance of promotion to the First Division. It was an important match for the home side as well. They needed a point to be sure of avoiding relegation back to the Third Division. For the first five minutes Oxford looked the stronger side but before long Carlisle began to dominate the match, though without being able to convert manifest superiority into even one goal. Only three minutes remained when Chris Balderstone floated a free-kick across the Oxford penalty area. Not for the first time, it was Bobby Owen whose thumping right-foot volley saved the day and secured both points for United.

The win at Oxford was crucial but Carlisle still needed to secure both points in the last match at home to Aston Villa and hope that other results would go their way. Blackpool were playing at Sunderland and Orient were away to Cardiff City. Blackpool had the same number of points as Carlisle but a better goal-average, so United needed to do better than the Seasiders. Orient were a point behind but also had a game in hand. They too had a superior goal-average, so Carlisle needed to do at least as well as Orient in terms of points earned in the remaining games of the season.

Aston Villa were usually another of Carlisle's nemeses and United had never beaten the Villa in their previous ten League and cup meetings. After the near-20,000 crowd for the Sunderland match, United were hopeful of a similar attendance for the Villa match. The gate, however, was a rather disappointing 12,494, although it was still the second highest League attendance of the campaign. It was also slightly higher than the 12,007 who turned out for the corresponding encounter at Villa Park a few weeks earlier. That match had attracted Villa's lowest gate for six years.

As for events on 27 April, Carlisle took an early lead through Joe Laidlaw's determined header from a knock-on by Bobby Owen. Fortune was again favouring Carlisle as twice Villa hit the woodwork, once following a save by Allan Ross who was having an outstanding game in goal. Having rode their luck in the first half, Frank Clarke made it two with another header midway through the second period to make the final score 2-0 to Carlisle. The victory pushed the Cumbrians up into third place and an automatic promotion place for the first time in the whole campaign.

United had done what they had to, but they were depending on the results from other games as the crowd waited on at the end of the match. Blackpool, who had needed to win to keep their own hopes alive, had lost at Sunderland, having held the lead for most of the match. Orient, meanwhile, had drawn at Cardiff and were now two points behind Carlisle but still with one game left to play. Orient also had a slightly superior goal-average to United so a win for them in their final fixture would push them above Carlisle to clinch that third place. Meanwhile, Carlisle and their supporters could only await their fate for the next six days.

Once again it was Aston Villa who held the key to United's fate. Their visit to Orient had originally been scheduled for early February but it was now scheduled to be the very last match in Division Two. The Orient fans turned out in force and a crowd of just under 30,000 squeezed into Brisbane Road to see if the O's could return to the First Division for the first time since their own season in the sun of 1962-63. Aston Villa, meanwhile, were lying a disappointing fourteenth in the table and had little to play for apart from their pride.

Pride, though, proved to be sufficient motivation, much to the delight no doubt of any Villa supporters who were present and, more importantly, the handful of Carlisle fans who were at the game. These included Allan Ross, Bill Green and Joe Laidlaw, and some of the directors who were combining a visit to the game with the chance to take in the FA Cup final the next day.

Though Bullock duly scored for the home side, a penalty by Villa's Ron Graydon ensured the game would end all square at 1-1. Orient, who had spent five consecutive months in the top three positions, ended the season in fourth place and Carlisle United, almost unbelievably, had come up on the rails to clinch promotion to the First Division.

CHAPTER 5

1974-75: Top of the League!

Looked at in the cold light of day, the achievement of Carlisle United in gaining promotion to the First Division was, to use a rather overworked phrase in this context, little short of incredible. United's fans are as loyal of those of any other club but in that promotion season the club's average gate was little more than 8,000. Only Hull City, rather surprisingly, and bottom of the table Swindon Town had lower crowds that season, while the best supported clubs such as Sunderland and Aston Villa would pull in average gates three times as big as Carlisle's. It is true that twelve years later Wimbledon reached Division One with an average attendance of barely 4,500 but then the Dons always were a special case. Their subsequent survival for fourteen years in the top flight was as much a footballing miracle as winning the FA Cup in 1988.

The Dons, though, were still in the Southern League when Carlisle made their own mark on history. With a population in the urban area of little over 70,000, Carlisle remains perhaps the smallest place to have hosted top division football since Glossop, who had a solitary season in the top flight in 1899-1900, during which they won a mere four matches. Wimbledon may have had small crowds but, situated in Greater London, they could hardly complain about their catchment area. Carlisle of course have always drawn a certain level of support from the surrounding rural area as well as West Cumberland but, even so, the ultimate crowd potential is always going to be limited.

It is sometimes said that the League table does not lie and it is a theory with which I tend to agree. Carlisle United finished in the third promotion place and were deservedly promoted, yet there is no denying that Carlisle's elevation to the First Division was not without an element of luck. Middlesbrough were clearly Division Two's dominant team in that season. Their total of 65 points from 42 games was the biggest in the League since Tottenham secured 70 over 50 years earlier. Not only that, but Boro ended the campaign fifteen points ahead of second-placed Luton. In the era of two points for a win, this was an all-time Football League margin. Had there been three points for a win, the gap would have been an even wider 23 points.

Luton Town meanwhile were runners up with 50 points from their 42 matches, which was the lowest total of any team finishing second since the First World War. Carlisle finished one place behind with one point fewer, but at least some teams – including the mighty Liverpool on one occasion – had earned fewer than Carlisle's 49 points in securing third place. Cleary it was not Carlisle's fault, in fact, but rather to their credit that they finished as high as third with such a modest points total. It must be admitted, however, that in choosing such a season to do so, their timing was as faultless as it had been in the final surge to clinch third spot in the very last match of the campaign.

Not that anybody minded as the city and its football team celebrated their huge achievement. 'Division One!' was the fairly obvious headline in the local paper, with the story subtitled 'Carlisle hit the big time'. For once, Fleet Street's finest also found the space to applaud the Cumbrians' achievement with the not-unexpected references to 'the shoestring club from Cumberland' 'Carlisle United, little Cumbrian outpost of League soccer' and perhaps more pleasingly 'the most romantic football story of the year'.

For a short period, the club was able to celebrate their achievement. A civic reception was held by the new Carlisle City Council that had come into existence only a month earlier. The players, along with Alan Ashman, Dick Young and chief scout Hugh Neil, paraded through the town in an open top bus on hire from Morecambe Corporation before taking the salute, as it were, from the balcony of the Civic Centre. There was a special cheer, too, for goalkeeper Allan Ross who had been at the club for eleven years. Rossie was the only player to have stayed continuously at Brunton Park from the Fourth Division to the First and his loyalty had just been rewarded with the award for Carlisle's Player of the Year. Not that the award was just for loyalty. Apart from the disaster at Luton, where the defence was caught square and conceded the six goals in twenty minutes, the United rearguard had been as solid as that of any other club in the League.

John Gorman had won the Player of the Year award for the previous two seasons and he had had another exemplary year at full-back. This time he finished in third place. The runner up to Allan Ross was Les O'Neill who had been in outstanding form in both defence and attack, as well as acting as the stand-in captain for a while in the autumn. The truth was that a case could have been made out for most of the team being given the award. In this day and age, when at least half a dozen Player of the Year awards of various kinds tend to be dished out at the end of the campaign, there would have been plenty of gongs to distribute for everybody. Perhaps Rossie was right when he promised to melt the trophy down and have eighteen miniatures made instead for every member of the squad.

Glory in football is however a very transient emotion, and it was not long before the club was having to face up to the realities of life in Division One. The demand for season tickets began almost as soon as promotion had been achieved, as Brunton Park was inundated with applications, even before the new prices were announced. In mid-May it was announced that the price of a centre-stand season ticket would rise from £14 to £24. The club pointed out in its defence that the previous season it had absorbed the introduction of VAT in its admission costs. Other prices rose, too, although supporters could still watch from the Warwick Road end or the Scratching Pen for a mere 50p (up from 40p) while the Paddock would now cost 60p per game (up from 45p). The rises were undeniably steep although viewed from today the costs seem modest. It was, after all, the chance to see the best football teams in the land.

One team that would not be making its way to Brunton Park in the forthcoming season was, of course, Manchester United. The Red Devils had never met Carlisle in either League or cup competition. Apart from Stoke City, (soon to be encountered) and newcomers Hereford and Cambridge, this made them unique among the other 91 League clubs. It was a meeting that would have to wait a while longer. At virtually the same time as Carlisle were celebrating their victory over Aston Villa on 27 April, Manchester United were dropping into the Second Division, courtesy of Denis Law, whose backheeled goal for Manchester City relegated his former club. As the two Uniteds were destined to change places again a year later, Carlisle have still never met Manchester United in the League although the two sides were drawn together in the FA Cup in 1978. As well as Manchester United, bottom club Norwich City were relegated, and the third club to go down was Southampton. It was the Saints whose misfortune it was to finish third from bottom and suffer the reverse fate of Carlisle.

This change in the composition of the First Division did not pass without comment, although the views expressed found little favour at Brunton Park. Malcolm MacDonald, centre-forward of Newcastle and not one of life's shrinking violets, commented that the presence of Carlisle United and indeed Luton Town would devalue Division One. A certain Kevin Keegan of Liverpool, who had plenty of experience of life at the bottom of the League with Scunthorpe, had similar thoughts, regarding Carlisle and Luton as a poor exchange for Manchester United and Norwich. Financially, no doubt, both players were correct but clearly 'the most romantic football story of the year' cut little ice with some.

Alan Ashman and his backroom staff, however, had more substantive issues to deal with and in particular the need to strengthen the team. The retained list, issued at the end of April, had given free transfers to defenders Stan Ternent and Brian Tiler. At the age of 27, Ternent should have been close to his football peak but his injury problems were beginning to take their toll and he never again played League football although Bob Stokoe took him to Sunderland. There he began a long career as a scout, coach and manager with a considerable number of clubs. Brian Tiler was some three years older than Stan Ternent and harboured his own ambitions as a coach and manager. His subsequent career would take him firstly to Wigan Athletic, who were then still a non-league outfit, and then via Zambia and the USA to Bournemouth where he became secretary and managing director. He was killed in a car crash in Italy during the 1990 World Cup.

Despite the influx of funds reflected by increased prices and the surge in season ticket sales, it was clear that, for a club that had always been careful to live within its means, United's buying power was very far from unlimited. Because the Carlisle team had been largely acquired through shrewd purchases from other lower division outfits, few of the players had experience of life in the top flight. In fact, the sixteen remaining members of the squad had made fewer than 140 appearances in total in the First Division, well over half of which (85) were attributable to Frank Clarke in his spells at QPR and Ipswich. At least Alan Ashman himself had spent four seasons as a Division One boss with West Brom.

It was no surprise, therefore, that Carlisle should be on the lookout for players who had featured in Division One. It was equally unsurprising that the first signing should come on a free transfer from a club far removed from the top flight. Eddie Spearritt's football career had begun with Ipswich Town, for whom he made nine First Division appearances in 1968-69 and rather more in Division Two in the three seasons before. He then moved south to Brighton where he eventually became club captain, a position he still held when Brian Clough arrived to manage the south coast club in November 1973. Having been outspoken in the local press over the turmoil following Clough's arrival, his days were numbered. 'We held a behind closed doors meeting and I emerged with a free transfer' is his recollection. 'I then had offers from seven clubs. Six of them guaranteed me first team football with teams in the Second, Third or Fourth Divisions. Carlisle gave me the chance to play First Division football and that was the attraction of the move.' Not that he had any doubts as to why he had been recruited. 'I knew that I had been signed as cover for the full backs or the sweeper.' So it was to prove, but at least Alan Ashman had begun to strengthen his undoubtedly modest squad. The main priority however was to acquire a central defender.

Bobby Parker was just seventeen when he made his first-team debut for Coventry City, his hometown club. By the summer of 1974 he had played 80 League games, all in Division One, for the Sky Blues where he normally featured in central defence. He had also captained the England Youth side in 1971 which won a tournament in Czechoslovakia. In his final term at Highfield Road, however, he lost his place and had recently spent more time in the Coventry reserve side. Alan Ashman had been aware of his potential from his own days in the West Midlands. Negotiations for his transfer were opened and early in June he joined Carlisle United for a club record fee of £52,500.

That sum made a big hole in the Carlisle transfer kitty but there was one more player to be recruited for the Division One campaign. Hugh McIlmoyle had been associated with Brunton Park since he first arrived from Rotherham in March 1963. Having been sold to Wolves eighteen months later – by which time he had become the Football League's top scorer – he later moved to Bristol City before returning to Carlisle in 1967 for a second spell.

In September 1969 he was sold to Middlesbrough, from whence he moved to Preston before returning to Scotland to play for his hometown club of Greenock Morton. While at Morton, he had been training at Brunton Park and had on occasions been linked to his favourite club. Finally the speculation became a reality. At the age of 34, his best days as a footballer were now behind him, but soon after Bobby Parker signed on the dotted line for Carlisle, so too did Hugh McIlmoyle who thus began his third spell at Brunton Park. 'He is 34 but has kept himself fit and trained here last season so we know what he can do' Alan Ashman opined. 'There will be competition for forward places next season.'

Off the pitch, too, progress was being made. Some ground improvements were required and at the Waterworks End the terracing was improved and an extra four rows of standing room added. More extensive works were put in place for the paddock, where the terracing was extended the full length of the pitch and retaining walls put in place. Season ticket sales had by mid-June reached £60,000, which was enough to pay for Bobby Parker, and the club also took steps to have its games sponsored.

To 'Rustproofing (Carlisle) Ltd' belongs the honour of being Carlisle's first match sponsors, when they had sponsored the Sunderland game in April. It was something of an experiment but the commercial potential was, with hindsight, obvious and by July the club announced it had secured sponsorship for nearly all the home games that season. First up were to be the brewers 'Courage' who had recently taken over a quarter of the pubs that had formerly belonged to the Carlisle and District State Management Scheme (of blessed memory).

In mid-July the players reported back for training, although some had already been in evidence at the ground, preparing themselves for the new campaign. Chris Balderstone had once again been given an exemption to fulfil his cricketing commitments but he too returned as agreed on 23 July. This concession had allowed him to play for Leicestershire in the Benson & Hedges Cup final in which he was his side's top scorer. Even he only reached 32 and, in a low-scoring game, Leicestershire lost to Surrey by 27 runs. Chris was still allowed to play in Sunday League games and his county eventually clinched the John Player Trophy, but for the last time in his sporting life, football was to be the first priority.

Carlisle United played no public friendlies as part of their preparation for the new campaign. The disorder that had accompanied the game against local rivals Workington was no doubt part of the reason. In contrast to Carlisle's ascent to the top rank of English football, the Reds were now hanging on to their Football League existence by their fingernails. Having endured another year of poor results and even poorer gates, their re-election ahead of Kettering Town had been secured by a mere five votes at the Football League's AGM. Notwithstanding these difficulties, Cumberland's two League clubs met for a couple of pre-season friendlies, both of which were won by Carlisle, their winning margins being 4-0 and 2-1. Joe Laidlaw bagged five of Carlisle's six goals and a few days later it was Chris Balderstone who scored in a 2-1 defeat in another closed doors encounter at Preston.

Carlisle's rise to Division One had helped them to secure an invitation to take part in the Texaco Cup. This competition had first been staged in 1970 and was originally given the less than snappy title 'International League Board Competition'. Luckily, Texaco stepped in as sponsors, which at least made the name less of a mouthful. The clubs who took part were English and Scottish ones without European commitments, and the early stages of the competition were organised on regional lines. Carlisle thus found themselves in a mini-league with the North East trio of Newcastle, Sunderland and Middlesbrough.

Carlisle's opener on 3 August 1974 took them to Middlesbrough's Ayresome Park. Boro, having been runaway champions of Division Two, were the undoubted favourites although they had made little effort to reinforce the team that had been so successful the previous term. United gave debuts to Bobby Parker and, for the third time in his career, Hugh McIlmoyle as they were able to field a virtually full-strength side with only Frank Clarke an obvious absentee. Boro, too, put out their first-choice eleven but it was Carlisle who emerged victorious, thanks to Dennis Martin's goal early in the second half. It was an encouraging performance against a side that had not lost at home in the League for almost a year. Particularly impressive were the performances of the veterans McIlmoyle and Balderstone, not to mention Allan Ross in goal.

Three days later, Newcastle United arrived at Brunton Park for the second game in the tournament. They too were at full strength and took the lead through winger Micky Burns. Carlisle's equaliser came from a surprising source. Mick Barry came on as a substitute and his raking drive from the edge of the area not only made the scores level but it marked his first ever goal in senior football. Four minutes from the end Joe Laidlaw's overhead kick put Carlisle ahead, only for Burns to snatch his second goal just before the end.

The draw nevertheless put United top of the group with just the home game to come against Sunderland the following Saturday. This time Mick Barry was on from the start but this time the 12,718 crowd, a few hundred down on the gate for the Newcastle fixture, witnessed a goalless draw, although arguably it was Sunderland who looked the likeliest to score. More galling, though, was the news that Newcastle had defeated Boro by 4-0. Under the rules of the Trophy, teams gained bonus points if they won by three or more goals. It was a repeat therefore of the outcome of the Anglo-Italian Tournament experience two years earlier when United had been denied by Blackpool's 10-0 victory over their Italian opponents. Newcastle, in fact, not only qualified for the quarter-finals of the trophy but also went on to successfully defend the cup they had won twelve months earlier.

Carlisle United therefore were eliminated despite being the only unbeaten team in their section, and were it not for the Magpies' bonus points, the Cumbrians would have topped the group. Yet despite the disappointment of losing out so narrowly, participation in the Texaco Trophy had been useful preparation for the coming campaign. It was Les O'Neill who pointed out the importance of gaining match practice before the start of any season and on that account the Texaco Cup had been very beneficial. Events were soon to show the prophetic nature of his remarks.

There were now only a few days to go before United played their opening fixture in Division One. Not only had season ticket sales smashed all records but, when the traditional pre-match photograph was taken, around 50 cameramen from all over the country were in attendance, rather than the usual handful from the local press and other agencies. The opening fixture of the season had pitted United against Chelsea at Stamford Bridge. Then as now, Chelsea were among the biggest spenders in the football world and had just recruited Celtic midfielder David Hay – who had starred in Scotland's World Cup campaign – as their new £225,000 signing. Another £50,000 had secured the services of winger John Sissons from Norwich City. The club had made headlines off the pitch as well, with the opening of their huge new East Stand, which itself cost £2 million and was at the time the biggest such edifice in the entire Football League.

A crowd of over 31,000 gathered at the Bridge on the afternoon of 17 August 1974 to witness Carlisle's historic first game in Division One. An estimated 2,000 visiting fans were there, as well as the *Match of the Day* cameras who watched the Chelsea team sportingly line up to applaud captain Bill Green lead the Carlisle team onto the pitch. After just 106 seconds into the game, he had put Carlisle into the lead, capitalising upon the home side's hesitation in failing to clear Chris Balderstone's curling free-kick. It was the quickest goal in the entire Football League. A quarter of an hour from the end, Les O'Neill made it 2-0 by chipping Peter Bonetti in the Chelsea goal. Whether it was intentional or a miskick mattered little to those of us watching in the cheaper seats in the West Stand. In between the two goals, United undoubtedly rode their luck as the home side twice hit the woodwork – once courtesy of Bill Green's attempted clearance – had shots cleared off the line and missed a crop of other chances, but by the final whistle Carlisle had won 2-0.

That victory over Chelsea remains one of the most famous in the club's history, aided no doubt by the fact that the game was captured for posterity on television that evening. Among the reporters at the game was Hunter Davies, who is regarded as one of Carlisle's few celebrity supporters. He had become famous as a football writer two years earlier with *The Glory Game*, a fly-on-the-wall account of life at Tottenham Hotspur in 1971-72. The book was revolutionary at the time through its depiction of life behind the scenes and is still in print, though today it would scarcely raise an eyebrow. Tottenham actually played against Carlisle in the FA Cup in that season. Curiously, this match is not referred to in the published book although there is a photo of the Spurs team arriving at Brunton Park.

The game against Chelsea at least gave Hunter Davies the chance to reaffirm his undoubted credentials as first and foremost a Carlisle supporter. His verdict on the match was 'Carlisle with far less individual skills [than Chelsea] played to their talent as a unit and produced pure football. Carlisle is good for football. Some good football, as we shall see this season, will come from Carlisle'. No United fan would disagree.

One Carlisle player above all would remember the Chelsea game for the rest of his life. Goalkeeper Allan Ross was the one member of the side who had remained at Carlisle all the way from the Fourth Division in 1963 through to Division One eleven years later. To him in particular, the victory at Chelsea was something special. 'Just to step out onto the field at Stamford Bridge, that was unbelievable and the highlight of my career' he later recalled. 'We were the country cousins, supposed to be the whipping boys for Chelsea and Bill Green scored the fastest goal of the season.' Allan Ross had recently celebrated a total of 350 League games for Carlisle and by the time he retired his total was 466, including rather bizarrely one substitute appearance as an outfield player at Portsmouth. In all he featured in well over 500 League and Cup games for the club. He remains easily the club's record appearance holder as well as being one of the most popular men ever to have played for Carlisle United.

As events were soon to demonstrate, Chelsea were far from the best side in the First Division that season, but it was still a remarkable performance by the Cumbrians. Alan Ashman too was aware that despite its significance, the Chelsea game would not be the most difficult his team would face that season. Three days later United were due to travel to Middlesbrough for a second visit in little over a fortnight. Boro had made an impressive start themselves, winning 3-0 at Birmingham and promised to provide a sterner test. But as Ashman realistically said before the Chelsea match: 'It's going to be hard and our First Division future may be uncertain ... but whose isn't?'

It was twenty years since Middlesbrough had last graced the First Division. Having won the Second Division title so convincingly, there was no lack of anticipation on Teesside over the coming campaign. To Carlisle, the Boro were familiar opponents. Not only had they met twice in the previous season but less than three weeks earlier Carlisle had come out on top when the two sides met in the Texaco Trophy. For this match, Dennis Martin came back into the starting line-up in place of Frank Clarke in the only change from the team that defeated Chelsea. This also meant that both sides lined up exactly as they had in the Texaco Trophy clash. The outcome was the same, too, except that instead of a 1-0 victory, Carlisle won 2-0, with both goals coming from midfielder Les O'Neill, who thus demonstrated that he without doubt was fully match fit.

'A little man with a big heart,' in the words of Allan Ross, O'Neill's two goals made him at the time the leading marksman in the First Division. In fact, along with Ken Wagstaffe of Hull City, who had made a similar start to the campaign, Les was at this point the top scorer in the whole Football League. For Les, as for the majority of his teammates, the Carlisle years were the best of his career. 'I always believed I could play and I liked the way we were coached and played the game. There was a great blend and team spirit in the side and I never played in another team like it.' Les performed something of a dual role in the side. Today he would be called a box-to-box player with his running and ball-winning skills, plus he liked to get into scoring positions and frequently did so. At Middlesbrough his first effort was a drive from within the penalty area. The second was a header from a cross by full-back Peter Carr that rounded off a five-man move. By the end of the game, even the Boro fans in the 28,719 gate were applauding United.

It was this result which first put Carlisle United on top of the League. On opening day the best result had been Manchester City's 4-0 win at home to West Ham. Stoke City and Middlesbrough had both posted 3-0 victories, which put all three clubs ahead of Carlisle. Defeats for Stoke and of course Boro on the Tuesday evening, plus Manchester City not playing, meant that Carlisle moved into first place, shading Ipswich Town through having scored four goals to their two. The next night Manchester City won again, beating Tottenham 1-0 to climb above the Cumbrians and back into top spot.

Tottenham had made a poor start to the campaign, losing at home to Ipswich on the opening day before the defeat at Maine Road. Now they were due to be the first visitors to Carlisle. Twice in recent seasons they had played at Brunton Park in the FA Cup and twice they had won, but defeat on this occasion was likely to leave them bottom of the League. Spurs had finished in mid-table in the previous campaign but their close season had been characterised by contract disputes with some of their leading players. They still, however, boasted a number of household names, including Pat Jennings and Martin Peters.

Carlisle, meanwhile, were forced to make one change. John Gorman's ankle injury had not healed, giving Tot Winstanley the chance to make his only League appearance of the season. Tot had been five years at Brunton Park following his transfer from Newcastle in the summer of 1969. Regarded as a 'players' player who always gave 100 per cent' in the opinion of Allan Ross, he was a regular in central defence in his first four years at the club. In the promotion campaign, following the signing of Bill Green, his first-team appearances became more spasmodic and at one point he asked for a transfer. When required, however, as when Bill Green was suspended at the end of the season and missed the final two games, he never let the side down and nor did he in the game against Spurs.

Carlisle's first home game in the top flight attracted a gate of 18,426, which while undeniably impressive, was actually the lowest in Division One that day. It was a useful reminder of the relatively limited resources available to the club compared to the rest of the League. United, though, took the fight to their illustrious opponents and after twenty minutes Joe Laidlaw was fouled inside the penalty area. Up stepped Chris Balderstone to take the spot-kick but Pat Jennings saved his shot. The referee, however, ordered a retake after ruling that the goalkeeper had moved before the kick was taken. This time there was no mistake as Balderstone's shot flew in high to the keeper's left. It proved to be the game's only goal and with Laidlaw in his most rampaging form, the score could easily have been greater.

Hugh McIlmoyle, on his own return to Brunton Park nearly five years after being sold to Middlesbrough, was warmly applauded when he was substituted towards the end. Carlisle had thus won their opening three games for the only time in their 100-year history. Manchester City, meanwhile, lost 0-4 at Arsenal, while Ipswich won 2-0 against Burnley. This gave the Tractor Boys three wins as well but with only four goals scored it left them one goal behind Carlisle who, it seemed almost impossible to realise, were top of the whole Football League. As the bookmakers slashed the odds on United winning the title from 200-1 to 33-1, Carlisle United savoured, for one heady weekend, the sensation of being the best team in the land.

The famous 24 August 1974 Division One League table (top half), which shows Carlisle United as the best team in England

FIRST DIVISION

	P		Home					Away				Pts
		W	D	L	F	A	W	D	L	F	A	
Carlisle	3	1	0	0	1	0	2	0	0	4	0	6
Ipswich	3	1	0	0	2	0	2	0	0	2	0	6
Liverpool ...	3	1	0	0	2	1	1	1	0	2	1	5
Wolves	3	1	1	0	4	2	1	0	0	2	1	5
Everton	3	1	1	0	2	1	1	0	0	3	2	5
Arsenal	3	1	0	1	4	1	1	0	0	1	0	4
Derby	3	1	1	0	3	1	0	1	0	0	0	4
Stoke	3	1	0	0	3	0	1	0	1	2	2	4
Man City ...	3	2	0	0	5	0	0	0	1	0	4	4
Middlesbrough	3	0	1	1	1	3	1	0	0	3	0	3
Chelsea	3	0	1	1	3	5	1	0	0	3	1	3

Joe Laidlaw in full cry against his old club as Carlisle and Middlesbrough meet at
Brunton Park in August 1974

Joe Laidlaw prepares to blast a free-kick in the same match,
as the Boro defence looks understandably nervous

Hughie McIlmoyle prepares to meet a cross against Middlesbrough in August 1974 at Brunton Park. Boro defenders Foggon, Souness and Boam also keep a watchful eye

Brunton Park, August 1974, as Chris Balderstone and Allan Ross are each presented with mementos to mark 350 senior appearances with the club

Bobby Owen, supported by Hughie McIlmoyle, outjumps the Liverpool defence in
October 1974

Les O'Neill attempts to round Luton goalkeeper Graham Horn in January 1974

Chelsea applaud Carlisle's players on to the Stamford Bridge in August 1974.
Joe Laidlaw leads out Peter Carr, John Gorman, Ray Train, Hughie McIlmoyle and
Chris Balderstone

Bobby Owen rejoices with the fans at the Waterworks End as Carlisle score against
Derby in October 1974

Chris Balderstone sets up Joe Laidlaw in the Fulham FA Cup-tie, March 1975

Bobby Owen strikes against Luton at Kenilworth Road in September 1973.
Frank Clarke looks on approvingly

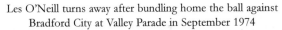

Les O'Neill turns away after bundling home the ball against
Bradford City at Valley Parade in September 1974

Les O'Neill prepares to shoot against Chelsea at Stamford Bridge in August 1974

Les O'Neill earns the congratulations from his old club as he leaves the field at
Bradford City in September 1974. Bobby Parker trots off looking well satisfied with the
result, while the ill-fated Main Stand at Valley Parade can be seen in the background

Chris Balderstone attempts to chip the Bradford City wall
in September 1974 at Valley Parade

Hughie McIlmoyle turns away in triumph after Les O'Neill scores Carlisle's second goal at Chelsea in August 1974 This was not a sight the occupants of the new East Stand were expecting to witness

Hughie McIlmoyle eludes the challenge of Liverpool's Alec Lindsey
at Brunton Park in October 1974

Derby keeper Colin Boulton saves from Bobby Owen at Brunton Park in October 1974

Frank Clarke and Chris Balderstone attempt to evade Derby's Peter Daniel in
October 1974 as Archie Gemmill looks on

Frank Clarke heads for goal against Leeds at Brunton Park in November 1974

Skipper Bill Green leads out the team against West Bromwich in the FA Cup-tie in January 1975. Allan Ross, as ever, is second in the line-up

No chance for former Luton keeper Alan Ross as Aston's goal flashes home

Second goal for Finney (left) and the third for Luton

Anderson (left) gets his second — number five for Town

How the *Luton News* gloried in Carlisle's nightmare at Kenilworth Road, as United concede six goals in the first half. For ex-Luton goalkeeper Allan Ross, it is one visit to his former club he will wish to forget. Carlisle lose to the Hatters for the first time ever

Back: M McCartney, F Clarke, P MacLachlan, A Ross, T Clarke, B Owen, M Barry,
Middle: H Nicholson (Physio), R Young (Coach), E Spearritt, D Martin, C Balderstone,
A Ashman (Manager), J Laidlaw, G Winstanley, H McIlmoyle, H Neil (Chief Scout).
Front: R Train, J Gorman, L O'Neill, B Green, P Carr, B Parker

More players run out against West Bromwich Albion in January 1975.
John Gorman is ahead of Dennis Martin and Bobby Owen

Joe Laidlaw takes the fight to Mansfield in the FA Cup-tie in February 1975

Mansfield keeper Rod Arnold gathers safely as Frank Clarke looks on
at Field Mill in February 1975

Luton's Jimmy Husband heads wide against Carlisle
at Kenilworth Road in September 1974

Bill Green challenges Fulham's John Lacy in the FA Cup-tie in March 1975

Hughie McIlmoyle, followed by Dick Young, leaves the field against Liverpool in October 1974

Allan Clarke (Leeds) and elder brother Frank leave the field together at Elland Road in February 1975. No prizes for guessing who is the happier

Allan Ross sportingly congratulates fellow goalkeeper and Fulham hero Peter Mellor after the FA Cup-tie in March 1975. Ray Train meanwhile keeps his thoughts to himself

Peter Carr (No 2) tries his luck against Fulham in the March 1975 FA Cup-tie

Defence in depth for Fulham as Bobby Moore (No 6) marshals his rearguard,
successfully as it turned out, against Carlisle in March 1975

Hughie McIlmoyle, in his last appearance for Carlisle, challenges
Luton keeper Keith Barber in March 1975

Frank Clarke, unmarked and in full flight, heads home against a
dispirited Everton in March 1975

January 1975 and Carlisle-born Kevin Beattie of Ipswich congratulates Joe Laidlaw (No 10) at the end of the game in which United defeat the League leaders at Brunton Park. Bobby Owen, meanwhile, looks less happy than might be expected

Dennis Martin is a study in concentration as he attempts to prise open the
Luton defence in March 1975 at Brunton Park

Luton exert pressure on the Carlisle rearguard in September 1974, as Bill Green,
Allan Ross and Bobby Parker prepare to defend the cause

Allan Ross has no chance as Jimmy Ryan converts from the spot for
Luton Town in September 1974

Joe Laidlaw flies through the air to head home against Luton Town at Brunton Park in
March 1975 before the lowest Brunton Park crowd of the season

Bill Green challenges Mick Lyons of Everton at Brunton Park in March 1975
as Peter Carr looks on

April 1975 and Chris Balderstone leaves the Brunton Park pitch for the last time after the defeat of Wolverhampton

Joe Laidlaw shows how to take a penalty against Everton in March 1975

There is no doubt about the outcome of the above penalty, as Frank Clarke and Les O'Neill move in to offer their congratulations

In his last game at Brunton Park in April 1975, Chris Balderstone shows he can still cut the mustard as he outwits the Wolverhampton defence

Not exactly *Swan Lake* as Bill Green and Ipswich's Bryan Talbot challenge for the ball at Brunton Park in January 1975

Making up for lost time. Eddie Prudham moves forward against Wolverhampton in April 1975 as he makes his first starting appearance for four months

Joe Laidlaw's acrobatics earn Carlisle an equalising goal against Luton Town in
September 1974

Joe Laidlaw tries to find a way through the Ipswich defence in January 1975.
Mick Mills moves across to try and block his attempt as Allan Hunter looks on

Bobby Parker (hidden) has his penalty attempt saved by Ipswich keeper Laurie Sivell in January 1975

Bobby Owen tries to penetrate the Ipswich rearguard in January 1975 but Mick Mills and Laurie Sivell have other ideas

Dennis Martin in the thick of the action against Ipswich Town in January 1975

Les O'Neill has Carlisle's second bite of the cherry in the twice-taken penalty against Ipswich in January 1975 but his shot flies wide, to the relief of keeper Laurie Sivell

CHAPTER 6

1974-75: Jousting with the Giants

Having reached the pinnacle of English football, it did not take Carlisle very long to discover that it was a lot harder to stay there. Carlisle's rise to the top of the League had confounded almost everyone and it is little wonder that the League table of 24 August 1974 is the most famous in the club's history. Three days later it was time to meet Middlesbrough again for the third time in less than four weeks. The two previous games had seen Carlisle twice come out on top at Ayresome Park but this time fortunes were reversed. David Armstrong scored for Boro after just two minutes and Carlisle never managed to get back onto level terms as they were frustrated by the Middlesbrough defence. At the same time Ipswich Town were defeating Arsenal 3-0 at Portman Road to keep their own 100 per cent record and displace United from the top of the table.

Despite the defeat by Boro, Carlisle remained near the top of the table. The bottom club was now Tottenham, and their poor performance prompted the resignation of manager Bill Nicholson. He it was who had guided Spurs to the double of Football League and FA Cup in 1961 when many people considered it to be an impossible feat. Tottenham defeated Leicester City to win the FA Cup final, when Hugh McIlmoyle first came to the attention of the football world when he was chosen ahead of Ken Leek to lead the Foxes' attack. Nor, of course, was he the only United player with a Leicestershire connection. Since 1971, Chris Balderstone had been a Leicestershire county cricketer. The forthcoming match at Filbert Street would, however, be the first time since moving from Yorkshire and Headingly to Leicestershire and Grace Road that he would have appeared there.

Leicester City had made an unspectacular start to the campaign and after only ten minutes Chris Balderstone and Joe Laidlaw combined to put in a cross that Hugh McIlmoyle steered home. It was only to be expected that Hughie would score against his former club and six minutes later Carlisle should have gone two up when Joe Laidlaw was fouled in the penalty area. The culprit was Graeme Cross, himself an occasional cricketer with Leicestershire, as well as a veteran of nearly 500 League games for the Foxes. Balderstone's penalty hit the outside of the post and the chance was lost. Five minutes from the end, a penalty for the home side enabled Frank Worthington to level the scores. The result still left Carlisle a very respectable fifth from the top. The new leaders, mean-

while, were now Liverpool who thus became the fourth side to top
Division One even though the campaign was just two weeks old.

Despite earning only one point, Carlisle were considered to have performed well at Leicester, especially in the first half when they could easily have been two or three goals to the good. Chris Balderstone in particular was warmly received by the home fans, while Hughie McIlmoyle's
Indian summer showed no sign of ending. 'At 34 I feel I can still do a job
for United. I certainly wouldn't want to keep my place here on sentiment',
he reflected soon after the Leicester game. 'I had a feeling our style of
play would be suited in this division and it seems to have been borne out.
Physical teams coming out of Division Two have often struggled whereas pure footballing teams have done well.'

It was surprising therefore to read that in some people's view a
'Carlisle crisis looms' after only one point from two games. Alan Ashman
for one was unimpressed. 'I exist on results and with seven points out of
ten ours have been good,' he maintained. 'I would rate it [the game at
Leicester] as our best First Division performance so far out of the five
matches we have played – certainly as good as the one we produced at
Middlesbrough.' Ashman's view of matters was confirmed the following
Saturday when it was announced that he had been chosen as the First
Division's Manager of the Month. It was the second time within a year
that the Carlisle boss had won such the award and while United had fall-
en from top spot by the end of the month, their achievement in even getting there from such low expectations made the Cumbrians' boss the
obvious choice.

The news came on the day that Stoke City arrived for their first ever
visit to Brunton Park. The Potters were a very good side, manager Tony
Waddington having fashioned a team that, like Carlisle, had gained a reputation for playing attractive football. In the previous campaign, the
Potters had finished fifth, high enough to qualify for European competition. Geoff Hurst was probably their best-known player, having joined
them from West Ham two seasons earlier, but injury kept him out of the
side that travelled to Brunton Park. The key figure in the Stoke line up
was, however, Alan Hudson, another refugee from the bright lights of
London, who had signed for the Potters in a club record £240,000 from
Chelsea at the start of the year. It was Hudson who dominated the game,
pulling the strings from midfield as well as scoring after only six minutes.
Centre-forward John Ritchie scored in the second half as the visitors won
rather more convincingly that the scoreline would suggest.

In the view of Dick Young, Stoke were as good a visiting side as he
had ever seen at Brunton Park, and having been there eighteen years he

had seen a good many teams. Bill Green was later to confirm that 'John Ritchie took me apart. He scored and at no time in the match did I solve how to either stop him getting the ball or getting it off him.' As for Alan Ashman, he confessed with admirable honesty: 'We could have employed a hatchet man to mark Alan Hudson but that is not our style. We laid up on him but he was too clever.' In truth, the real problem that Carlisle were finding was the lack of a cutting edge in front of goal, a weakness that was to haunt them throughout the season. In three home games, Carlisle had managed to score only once and that from a twice-taken penalty. Just one goal in the six games had come from a recognised forward and the top scorer was midfielder Les O'Neill. The defence, in contrast, had performed well, conceding only four goals in the first six games. Despite an average age of only 22, the back four of Bill Green, Bobby Parker and full-backs Peter Carr and John Gorman had generally played with an assurance that belied their years. The two centre-backs in particular had fashioned an effective partnership, Bill Green's aerial dominance being complemented by Bobby Parker's work on the deck.

Four days after the Stoke defeat, Carlisle travelled to Fourth Division Bradford City for a second round League Cup-tie. It was one of Les O'Neill's former clubs and predictably it was only his goal that separated the two sides at the end. For the next game, away to Newcastle, Les was given the honour of captaining the side against the club he supported as a boy. A huge contingent of Carlisle supporters made the short journey across to St James' Park and gallingly witnessed John Tudor score the only goal for the Magpies just two minutes from the end.

The game at Newcastle had been tight, and Carlisle paid the price for their one lapse in concentration just before the end. Conceding a late goal was unfortunately to become something of a recurring theme as the campaign progressed. On this occasion it meant the end of Carlisle's unbeaten away record but despite some good work from McIlmoyle, Laidlaw and the returning Frank Clarke, the forwards had again failed to get among the goals. Clarke had not featured much in the season's early games. The outstanding form of Hugh McIlmoyle had made him the first choice to lead the line and this had prompted the former Ipswich man to request a transfer, a plea that the club refused. Mick Barry, too, was not happy at still being sidelined for the most part, though he had featured against Stoke City.

Carlisle continued to make news, however, and September saw the release of the first ever record to be inspired by the club's achievements. *Looking Good we're Carlisle United* was written by Tim Barker and Andrew Titcombe, both formerly of Nelson Thomlinson School, along with

London-based John Murphy. The tune is loosely based on that of *John Peel* and the song performed by 'Tim Barker and the Carlisle United Singers'. For those who may not have heard it, the chorus goes:

'Carlisle United, the team that's on the ball
    Carlisle United, the team for one and all
You're looking good and we're with you all the way
    You'll hear us singing every time you play'

Literature too was making its mark as the start of the season saw the publication of *The Carlisle United Story: Shaddongate to Division One*, written by Ronald Cowing, Martin Lawson, and Bill Willcox. It was the first attempt to chronicle the club's history from its origins in 1904 right up to the start of the First Division season.

The day of the Newcastle match saw Ipswich return to the top of the table with a 4-1 victory at Luton, while Liverpool lost at Manchester City. Also defeated were Derby County who went down 2-3 to Birmingham City. Lying fourteenth, with only one win in their first seven matches, the Rams were hardly looking like potential champions.

Nor by this stage were Carlisle United, although they were still lying in ninth place after the defeat by Newcastle. Seven days later United were back on the winning trail with a victory over Birmingham City at Brunton Park. Despite the presence of Joe Laidlaw, Hugh McIlmoyle and Frank Clarke in the United line-up, once again the goalscorer was midfielder Les O'Neill, and again a penalty-kick played its part. Chris Balderstone took the kick that was awarded after a foul on McIlmoyle but, though it was saved, Les O'Neill was the quickest to slot home the rebound:

'The goals to me are just a bonus,' he modestly explained later. 'I'm basically a midfield man whose main job is to make the chances for my team mates. I've managed to work myself into shooting positions and I've been lucky enough to put some of these chances away.' The visitors were down to ten men after this as full-back Archie Styles was dismissed for dissent, but the score remained 1-0 to Carlisle. Three days later Manchester City also failed to score on their own visit to Brunton Park but so too did Carlisle. Three points from the two home games did, how-ever, stop the rot as Carlisle prepared to travel to Luton, themselves also newly promoted from last season but so far without a win.

Luton Town were bottom of the League when Carlisle travelled there at the end of September. Despite being without a victory, they had only dropped to the bottom during the week, when they had lost to Coventry City, themselves winless until defeating the Hatters. Carlisle of course were keen to banish the memory of twelve months earlier when they had lost 1-6. It was a particularly sore point for goalkeeper Allan Ross. His professional career had begun at Kenilworth Road and until that defeat he had never lost to Luton in eight games. Apart from being bottom of the league, Hatters fans woke to the news that their star striker Barry Butlin was about to join Nottingham Forest. Carlisle, meanwhile, fielded the same eleven who had drawn with Manchester City.

In his regular column in the *Evening News & Star*, Rossie had singled out Peter Anderson as a Luton dangerman. Perhaps the rest of the team did not read what he wrote, as after just twelve minutes it was Anderson who put Luton ahead. Joe Laidlaw grabbed his first goal of the season with an overhead kick from a McIlmoyle knockdown to equalise, before Adrian Alston stumbled through some unusually half-hearted tackling to put the home side ahead. Alston had made his name in that summer's World Cup tournament in which he had represented Australia, despite being born in Preston. A third goal from the penalty-spot after handball was given against Bobby Parker made it a miserable day out for Carlisle and their fans. To complete a wretched weekend, it was announced that John McGovern, for whom Carlisle had made a record bid to Leeds United, had decided to stay at Elland Road. A Brian Clough signing during his short managerial spell at Leeds, McGovern eventually followed his mentor to Nottingham Forest with whom he was to win the European Cup some years later. With hindsight therefore, he probably made the right decision.

Carlisle, meanwhile, now had to face the visit of Liverpool. The FA Cup holders were under new management after Bill Shankly's dramatic retirement during the summer. Bob Paisley, his wily successor, was still a relatively unknown quantity and certainly not expected to eclipse his predecessor's achievements in terms of trophies won, though in due course he would do so. The *Match of the Day* cameras were also in town for the game, which was expected to attract a 20,000 crowd. The television agreement with the BBC that year was that every First Division club should host at least one *Match of the Day* and this match proved to be Carlisle's only such opportunity. The Reds were no strangers to Brunton Park. In each of the two previous campaigns they had played in cup-ties against Carlisle but they remained, along with Leeds United, easily the biggest draw in the League as a visiting team.

As for the game itself, it followed a familiar pattern, with Carlisle matching their famous opponents in everything except finishing power. Dennis Martin in particular had an exceptional match, posing a constant threat to the Reds' defence. It was to no avail, as Ray Kennedy punished a moment of slackness to score the only goal. At least the crowd forecast proved to be accurate, as the game attracted 20,844, which remains United's highest ever gate for a League match. More worryingly though, the result pushed Carlisle into the bottom half of the table for the first time. The strength of the Carlisle squad was also about to be tested as Ross, McIlmoyle and Laidlaw all picked up injuries.

Four days afterwards Carlisle made the long journey to Colchester for their third round League Cup-tie. As well as the three players injured on the Saturday, Chris Balderstone and Mick Barry were both also unavailable and Les O'Neill was doubtful. Colchester were near the top of the Third Division and proud of the fact that they had never lost at home to a First Division side in the cup. Carlisle, meanwhile, were forced to field a changed side. Tom Clarke played in goal, Tot Winstanley came in for Les O'Neill in midfield, and Eddie Spearritt also made his first appearance. The game stayed goalless until Dennis Martin made a fatal error with an intercepted back-pass. Soon afterwards a penalty gave the home side a rather flattering victory, while Carlisle had the rare experience of being on the wrong end of a giant-killing.

It was the second General Election of 1974 the following day. I remember choosing not to travel from West London out to Colchester because I was on duty early the next morning as a presiding officer in one of the Hounslow constituencies. The Carlisle team, meanwhile, had decided not to exercise their democratic right at all. Three days after the game at Colchester, Carlisle were due to play at Wolverhampton and Alan Ashman decided it would be more sensible if the team stayed in the south until after the Wolves game. 'I explained the position to the players and made it clear that if anyone wanted to vote then we would come home after the Colchester game. No one raised any objections, in fact one player said it would probably make no difference as their votes would cancel each other out.' For the record it should be recorded that Ron Lewis was re-elected as MP for Carlisle by a rather bigger margin than the size of the Carlisle United party in Colchester.

Chris Balderstone was fit to return for the Wolves game. Tom Clarke, though, was given his chance in goal while Hugh McIlmoyle missed the opportunity to play against his former club. Eddie Spearritt kept his place to make his Division One debut for Carlisle. Wolves won 2-0 with the second goal a long-range effort from full-back Derek Parkin.

Four days later Carlisle were on their travels again, this time back to London and Tottenham Hotspur. Spurs were now bottom of the League, the resignation of Bill Nicholson having made little difference to their fortunes. Allan Ross returned to the side, to the disappointment of Tom

Clarke, who had performed well in his two outings. Mick Barry, too, was back in the starting line-up and after four minutes his pass set up Bobby Owen to put Carlisle ahead. It was, as I recall, a wet October night and the crowd of 12,823 was the lowest at White Hart Lane for some years. Tottenham equalised through Martin Chivers just before half-time but the 1-1 draw continued Carlisle's unbeaten run in the capital.

Goals, though, were still hard to come by for Carlisle, particularly at Brunton Park where the six home games had still only produced two goals, both resulting from penalties. Derby County were the next team due at Brunton Park. Since losing to Birmingham in mid-September, their form had improved to the extent they were now lying fourth from top. For once, however, it was Carlisle who took their chances as Ray Train and Dennis Martin and Frank Clarke all got their names on the scoresheet for the first time all season. It was to prove Carlisle's best win all season, yet ironically it was done without several first-choice players, as Allan Ross, Les O'Neill, Hugh McIlmoyle and Joe Laidlaw were all still absent through injury.

The win over Derby was a valuable confidence-booster. It still left Carlisle, however, below halfway in the table and coincidentally just one place above their next opponents. It is a curious fact that Carlisle and Coventry have only ever spent five seasons in the same division but the meetings encompass the former First, Second, Third and even the Fourth Division in 1958-59. In that term, Coventry won 6-1 at Brunton Park, though Carlisle in turn managed to secure both points in the reverse fixture at Highfield Road. This time, it was the turn of Bobby Parker to be captain for the day and to lead the team out at Coventry against his former club and hometown side. The game itself was fairly even, which by now was tending to mean that Carlisle matched their opponents everywhere but inside the penalty area. So it proved again, with Frank Clarke's opportunist goal being trumped by two Coventry efforts from set pieces, both of which were credited to centre-half Larry Lloyd. As a result of that defeat, Carlisle dropped one more place as Coventry moved one rung above them. Liverpool, meanwhile, had returned to the top spot as Ipswich's run of two points from six games had pushed them down to third in the table.

The defeat at Coventry's Highfield Road was followed by another away trip, the fourth in five matches, this time to Sheffield United. The Blades were then managed by ex-Workington boss Ken Furphy who had joined them the previous December. The club was known to have financial problems but they had made a useful start to the season, having already beaten Ipswich and Liverpool, and were lying just above halfway.

Tom Clarke continued in goal for the injured Allan Ross but his fail-ure to hold an early cross allowed the home side to take the lead. Two minutes later the Blades scored again, though this time the keeper could not be blamed. Hugh McIlmoyle, who had been on the bench for the Coventry match, had returned and he pulled a goal back with a fine head-er from a Peter Carr cross. It was Hughie's last ever goal for Carlisle, so it was appropriate that it should have been one of those typically flash-ing headers that had delighted Carlisle fans for so many years.

West Ham were Carlisle's next opponents, making their first and only visit to Brunton Park. The one previous meeting between the two clubs had been an FA Cup-tie in 1910, when both the first game and the replay had been played at Upton Park. On paper it looked to be one of the most attractive games of the season but a strong wind and a rain-soaked pitch made conditions difficult – though Trevor Brooking, for one, was able to overcome them as he dominated the match. The outcome was, though, predictable, as Frank Lampard scored the only goal early in the second half with a twenty-yard drive from a ball that was not properly cleared. Once again United were punished for a defensive lapse yet even now only Ipswich and Liverpool had better defensive records than Carlisle. Sadly, only Luton had a poorer scoring one. As for the top of the table, it was now the turn of Manchester City to return to first place after their victo-ry over Stoke.

Alan Ashman, though, was keeping as calm as could reasonably be expected. 'I have been a manager for twelve years and have faced a run like this many times before. I told the team at the start of the season that we should not develop any inflated ideas about the ability of our side. Unless you've got a team like Leeds or Liverpool you have got to keep level headed about a bad run.' At least Carlisle's injury problems were clearing up and for once the full squad looked to be available for the next game.

Financially, life in Division One was going to be different but so far this side of things at least was going to plan. The club had budgeted for an average gate of 14,000 and to date it was 17,000. This was partially off-set by the fact that away attendances were averaging fewer than 26,000, compared to the budgeted figure of 28,000. Overall though, the projec-tions were positive as secretary David Dent put it: 'We have our home fans to thank for their response to our entry to the First Division. The increase in home game receipts far outweighs the decrease in away games.' The results from the previous year, however, made for less happy reading as the club reported a loss of £106,000, including a deficit on transfer activity alone of £92,000. Although gate receipts had risen by

£16,000, wages were £33,000 higher. At least the supporters club continued to flourish and their £14,000 contribution helped to reduce the overall loss.

It was the turn of Stan Bowles to be made captain for the day when
Carlisle travelled to play Queens Park Rangers, who had lost 2-5 at Derby
the week before. Allan Ross was restored to the goalkeeping slot, while
Joe Laidlaw was fit again and replaced Hugh McIlmoyle. Once again
Carlisle lost 1-2, but for once the score flattered United. Predictably Stan
Bowles was among the scorers, while Carlisle's consolation effort was a
penalty by Bobby Parker who had now taken over spot-kick duty. That
defeat, moreover, pushed Carlisle down to second from bottom with only
Luton Town below them.

Despite making three close-season signings, the club was continuing
to try and recruit new players to strengthen the squad. Chief scout Hugh
Neil was taking in several games a week to assess players. The matches he
would watch for this purpose were seldom Division One games as the
players would be out of Carlisle's financial reach. Recently he and Alan
Ashman had made several visits to Partick Thistle but while the purpose
of the visit was to check on the home team's own players, they were also
fielding a forward on loan from Sheffield Wednesday. Eddie Prudham
was just 22 but had been at Hillsborough for several years without really
breaking into the first team. On loan to the Jags, he had scored in three
successive games. The Carlisle view was that he had potential and he was
signed for a £35,000 fee. As Prudham arrived, Tot Winstanley, who had
been on loan to Brighton, joined them in a £20,000 deal.

Eddie Prudham made his debut against Leeds United the following
weekend, coming in for Chris Balderstone. The crowd of 19,975 was
among the best of the season and they witnessed Dennis Martin giving
Carlisle an early lead against the reigning League champions. For the rest
of the half Carlisle dominated but once again they failed to turn their
superiority into goals. Soon after half-time Joe Jordan sneaked in on the
blind side to equalise, then five minutes from the end Duncan McKenzie
snatched the winner to hand out another harsh lesson to the home side.
It was the fifth consecutive one-goal defeat but as Johnny Giles commented: 'I have never been here before and I was staggered at Carlisle's
show. They did it all didn't they? For some time in the game we did not
know where we were. But we won. We have the experience you see.' Even
more telling was the tale recounted after the game to Allan Ross by Billy
Bremner, the Leeds captain. Apparently, one of the Carlisle team had
apologised to him after he had been fouled. To Bremner, this was a most
unprofessional attitude.

Having just faced the reigning champions, Carlisle's next fixture involved the longest journey of the season to the team many felt could be the next to win the title. Under manager Bobby Robson, Ipswich Town had been in the top four all season and in Carlisle-born Kevin Beattie, they possessed potentially one of the outstanding footballers in the country. Mick Barry was drafted in for this game, replacing Joe Laidlaw who took his place on the bench, and it was Frank Clarke who led the side out against his former team. Within two minutes Town had taken the lead, having already had another goal disallowed for offside. A second goal followed before half-time as Carlisle looked a well-beaten side. The second half was a different story, as that man Les O'Neill cracked home a twenty-yard shot to put United back in the game, but the home defence, with Beattie outstanding, held firm. Late on, the home side scored again for a 3-1 victory, although the attendance of 20,122 was the lowest of the campaign at Portman Road. The win pushed Ipswich back up to second place but by now Stoke City were the new leaders and the fifth team to top the table that season.

After the match it was the turn of Bobby Robson to pay tribute to the visitors. 'Carlisle are a credit to the First Division. They didn't come here to close it up and defend, they came to play and they allowed us to play.' It is easy, of course, to be magnanimous in victory but these sentiments were little different to Ashman's own view: 'I was not disheartened by the game. I was told by the Ipswich people that no team has come to Portman Road this season and made more goalscoring chances than we did. We made mistakes in defence. We would have recovered from that if the chances had been rapped in. There was no shortage of people appreciating our play. We don't kick. We don't close up tight. We don't shut up at the back playing a back four and a sweeper behind them. I don't want to do this. I believe we can get results by honest attacking football.'

Ashman's philosophy was, however, to be tested in Carlisle's next match, at home to Arsenal. The Gunners had been struggling all season and had even been bottom of the table at one point. In fact, improbable as it may seem from today's perspective, at one point in the season the three bottom clubs were Arsenal, Chelsea and Tottenham. Arsenal, though, were still the Arsenal, one of the most famous names in English football and the attendance of only 12,926 was a definite disappointment to the United management. Carlisle decided to stick with the eleven players who had featured at Ipswich and it was Eddie Prudham who opened his account with an early headed goal to give Carlisle the lead. Dennis Martin added a second before a late Brian Kidd effort gave Carlisle a nervous last few minutes before recording a 2-1 victory.

The win briefly moved United back up one place, and after six consecutive defeats it was a more than welcome result. Just as important, however, in the view of many spectators was the manner of the home team's victory. While Arsenal's results had improved of late, it was clear they had set out to intimidate Carlisle and soon after their second goal a mass brawl broke out. 'During the half time break, the boss warned us about keeping our cool because we could all sense a real flare up in the second half,' Frank Clarke admitted later: 'The character of our players showed through when they refused to retaliate despite massive provocation by the opposition.' 'My players don't go looking for trouble, they play football and will continue to do so,' was Alan Ashman's comment on the encounter. The question was, though, whether playing football alone would keep Carlisle in the top flight.

The victory over Arsenal brought Carlisle's season to its halfway point. After the brilliance of the early start that had propelled them to the top of the League, results had clearly been less than favourable. The club had gradually dropped down the table and the run of six straight defeats was something of a disaster. Yet following the win over Arsenal, United might have been third from bottom, but were only twelve points behind Stoke City who were top of the League. Luton Town, in bottom place, were six points below Carlisle, while Sheffield United, six points higher than the Cumbrians, were in the top half of the table.

The situation, then, was far from hopeless as a poll of other coaches and managers tended to confirm. Jimmy Armfield of Leeds was the most positive and Bob Stokoe at Sunderland certainly hoped that Carlisle would stay up. Others, such as Ian McFarlane and Frank Clark the captain of Newcastle United, were less sanguine. They acknowledged that Carlisle were respected for their style of football but also that a side needed to get the breaks. Carlisle had probably used more than their share of luck in beating Chelsea on the opening day of the season. Another large slice of luck in the forthcoming visit of Chelsea to Brunton Park would therefore not come amiss.

CHAPTER 7

1974-75: The Turning of the Tide

Four months after they had travelled to Stamford Bridge for that historic opening game in Division One, it was United's turn to play host to Chelsea in the return. Chelsea had begun the season with high hopes, not just because they looked to have a straightforward home fixture to start the campaign, but the opening of the new East Stand seemed to symbolise the beginning of a new era at the Bridge, a ground that in truth had seen better days. Things had not quite turned out as planned and by the time they travelled north to Brunton Park, the Pensioners had won only four League games. Manager Dave Sexton had lost his job in October, and Chelsea were lying just one place and one point above United. Carlisle meanwhile kept the faith with the eleven who had defeated the Arsenal.

At Stamford Bridge it had been Carlisle who had taken the lead after two minutes, after Bill Green had got the better of Mickey Droy the Chelsea centre-half and man-mountain. This time, fortunes were completely reversed. It took just three minutes for Droy to win a free-kick duel with his Carlisle counterpart to set up John Hollins who put Chelsea ahead. Hollins scored a second goal midway through the first half, although not before Dennis Martin had hit an opportunist equaliser from the edge of the penalty area. There was no further score and Carlisle's defeat pushed them back down to second from bottom. Meanwhile, Everton became the latest team to top the table after their 1-0 victory at Derby.

Things were not looking so good off the pitch either for United as they had two more transfer requests to deal with from unsettled players. Two days before the Chelsea match Bobby Owen asked for a move. It had been a frustrating season so far for the versatile forward. Having been an automatic choice in the promotion campaign, he had lost out to Hughie McIlmoyle in the early team selection and had made just a handful of starts, with just the one goal scored at Tottenham. At the age of 27 he should have been at his peak and was not the first player to be frustrated by the lack of a reserve side, a situation in which Carlisle were unique among Division One clubs.

Shortly afterwards Joe Laidlaw also requested a transfer. Having been the club's only ever present in 1973-74, he had lost his place through injury following the Liverpool game. Although he was restored to the side when fit, he had been dropped after the Leeds match. Like Bobby Owen, he had found goalscoring a problem and so far had found the net just once.

Injury worries, too, were compounding Carlisle's problems. Eddie Prudham had been carried off in the Chelsea game and was rated doubtful for the next match, while Mick Barry suffered an injury in training the following week. Prudham, of course, had had little chance to make his mark but Mick Barry had been starting to show the form that had originally persuaded Carlisle to pay £35,000 for his signature eighteen months earlier. Injury problems had caused him to miss most of the promotion campaign but latterly he had begun to enjoy a more settled run in the side, mainly at the expense of Chris Balderstone. Barry had lost weight and given up smoking in a serious bid to increase his level of fitness and realise his undoubted potential. Although he was born in Hull, Mick Barry was also qualified to play for Wales not, as might cynically be supposed, through his surname, but by dint of his father who came from Newport. The prospect of representing the land of his father had fuelled his son's ambitions and this latest injury was less than welcome to all concerned.

Not least, this was because Carlisle were next due to visit the new leaders Everton at Goodison Park. Without setting the world alight, the Toffees had so far lost only one game in the campaign. Were it not for the fact that over half of their matches had finished all square, their lead would have been much more commanding but in Bob Latchford they possessed one of the most prolific strikers in the division. Goodison Park would also be a new venue for United, as although the two sides had been drawn together in cup-ties, the two previous meetings in 1930 and 1968 had both been at Brunton Park. With Messrs Barry and Prudham unavailable, their misfortune allowed Joe Laidlaw and Chris Balderstone to come back into the reckoning in what proved to be one of Alan Ashman's more fortunate team selections. Hughie McIlmoyle, meanwhile, took Balderstone's place on the substitutes bench, while among the 33,489 crowd was Bill Shankly who was watching Carlisle for the first time that season.

He had barely settled in his seat when Bob Latchford gave Everton the lead after six minutes. Early in the second half he made it 2-0 as Carlisle looked dead and buried. Yet within five minutes United were level with two goals from the recalled Joe Laidlaw. First he headed home Peter Carr's cross from a clever Balderstone reverse pass, then struck home from 30 yards after John Gorman's long through-ball was not properly cleared. Finally, Chris Balderstone set up the winner with a perfect cross for top scorer Les O'Neill to head home. The Goodison side surged forward to try and equalise but for once the United rearguard held firm and Carlisle pulled off a marvellous and unexpected victory. 'They were magnificent' enthused Shankly. 'This was a great display and I enjoyed it very much.'

For Joe Laidlaw the result was a vindication of his, perhaps, rather fortuitous return to the side. 'It is really good to be recalled to the first team even though I felt I didn't deserve to be dropped,' he commented after the game. 'We all like to score goals but getting those two against Everton was great. But don't ask me to live through many more spells like those twenty minutes when they threw everything at us.' Laidlaw's performance was a vindication for someone else as well. Dick Young had been calling him back in the afternoon for extra training and to improve his fitness levels. He also felt that he was carrying too much weight. 'He is a player with a lot of ability,' was Dick's judgement 'and a lot of room for improvement. He can go on to become an outstanding footballer by using his strength, shooting power and aggression but he has to be in the right frame of mind.' It was a typical example of Dick Young seeing the scope for improvement in a player and working with him to bring out that potential.

Dick Young and his philosophy remained a vital element of Carlisle United and their style of play, with its emphasis on 'push and run' and playing good football. 'Our brand of football is the key to our survival,' he mused while surveying Carlisle's position near the foot of the table. 'In my time here we have got out of the Second, Third and Fourth Divisions playing football that creates goalscoring chances. That football also kept us in each higher division and I feel, even when things look as they do now, that is the key. We are novices at this level. It is our lack of experience that has caused us problems. We must be tighter at the back and take more chances up front. Fortunately our football style in general has not been forgotten.'

For Allan Ross, too, the game was rather special, despite conceding two goals to the home side. The Goodison fixture was his 377th League match for Carlisle United, which at the time was regarded as setting a new appearance record for the club. Or, rather, technically it did not. Ron 'Ginger' Thompson played 376 League games for Carlisle between 1951 and 1964, which was the previous highest total for the club. Two of those matches however were against Accrington Stanley in 1961-62, the season they dropped out of the Football League. These games were later expunged from the records after Stanley's demise to reduce Ron's total to 374. Therefore Rossie actually broke his record in the win over Arsenal two weeks earlier. Over 30 years later, Rossie's record looks as secure as ever, as he eventually turned out in 466 League matches for the club, none of which were later expunged from the records.

The unexpected Christmas present of the win over Everton at least put the club in good heart for the Boxing Day visit of Newcastle. The match was among the most keenly anticipated all season, with the proximity of Newcastle and the fact that it had been scheduled for Boxing Day. The Carlisle players in particular were looking forward to the encounter, especially those such as Les O'Neill, the former trainee with the Magpies and Bill Green who had grown up in the shadow of St James' Park. The capacity of Brunton Park was now officially set at 28,000 after the ground improvements during the summer and there was a real expectation that a new attendance record would be established. The game was made all-ticket but, perhaps surprisingly, the eventual gate of 20,675 was slightly below that for the Liverpool encounter a few weeks earlier. Over 7,000 tickets remained unsold, though had sales on the day been allowed, a higher gate would undoubtedly have been recorded.

Frank Clarke was injured, so Hugh McIlmoyle returned to the side with Bobby Owen on the bench. The Magpies, meanwhile, paraded their latest big-money signings in Geoff Nulty from Burnley and Tommy Craig – later, of course, to feature in Carlisle's colours – from Sheffield Wednesday. The visitors took a first-half lead through John Tudor, whose late strike had dashed Carlisle's hopes at St James' Park. Near the end, Bobby Owen pounced on a defensive error to equalise, but two minutes from time Newcastle grabbed another late winner. Malcolm MacDonald surged through the Carlisle defence, brushing aside several challenges. I can still picture his unstoppable run as he buried his shot past a helpless Allan Ross and into the Carlisle net. MacDonald's autobiography was entitled *Never Afraid to Miss* but on that occasion at least his aim was straight and true.

Two days later Carlisle travelled to Burnley for their last game of 1974. United were still second from bottom, although Luton Town were belatedly showing signs of life, having won at Ipswich while Carlisle were going down to Newcastle. Burnley, meanwhile, were continuing to confound the critics by demonstrating that a small-town club could survive in the top flight. For this game, Mike McCartney was called up for his full debut, replacing the injured John Gorman at left-back. Dennis Martin put Carlisle in the lead with a typically neat opportunist chip over a goalkeeper standing just a yard too far forward off his line. The Clarets equalised early in the second half but again Carlisle's concentration let them down in the last minute, allowing Collins to snatch the winner.

Once more Carlisle had dominated large periods of the game only to end up with nothing.

At least the FA Cup would provide a distraction from what was obviously going to be a stiff battle against relegation. The third round draw had given Carlisle an away tie against Preston North End. Last season the two clubs had both been in the Second Division, but now two divisions separated them. The Lilywhites were holding their own in the Third Division, aided by the presence on the pitch of Bobby Charlton who had decided to play for the side as well as manage it. Carlisle, meanwhile, had painful memories of their two previous cup visits to Deepdale. In 1964, United had travelled there as a Fourth Division side for a fifth round FA Cup-tie and had lost 0-1 on a day when Second Division Preston had seemed to get all the breaks. Preston then marched all the way to the final before losing to West Ham. Two years later, Carlisle had met Shrewsbury Town in a fourth round second replay at Deepdale. Deep into injury-time, Carlisle were winning 2-1 when the Shrews snatched a last-minute equaliser before going on to win 4-3 in extra-time. A young Frank Clarke was playing for Shrewsbury in those days and he had been one of the goalscorers.

This time, fortunes were reversed. Playing in front of an 18,682 gate, Preston's best crowd of the season, Carlisle won 1-0 without looking anything like a First Division outfit. It was Joe Laidlaw, featuring this time as the central striker, whose opportunist effort after half an hour made the difference between the two teams. Bill Green at centre-half was a tower of strength but the real hero for United was Allan Ross. Playing his best game for months, he denied Bobby Charlton, Tony Morley, Mel Holden and others with a string of fine saves. Charlton himself was quick to praise Rossie for his contribution to the result. 'We could have had a replay if Ross in their goal had not been playing so well. We made the chances and he stopped us taking them.' By the end of the 90 minutes, Carlisle had at least demonstrated they could play badly and win, as opposed to the more usual story of playing well and losing.

The win at Preston put United into the fourth round where they were drawn at home to the winners of a replay between West Brom and Bolton Wanderers. For Alan Ashman, however, the news was of little significance. 'Every match from now on is important and Saturday's at Highbury doubly so. What we need is to string three results together. They are all tough games in the First Division and you couldn't ask for a harder task than trying to get four points from our next two games away to Arsenal and home to Ipswich. We are forgetting all about the Cup for the time being.'

One of the attractions of the 1974-75 season for travelling supporters was the chance to see Carlisle United in unfamiliar surroundings. In
all, Carlisle met nine of the other 21 teams for the first time in League as
opposed to cup competition. For five of those nine teams – the London
trio of Arsenal, Tottenham and West Ham, and the Merseyside pair of
Everton and Liverpool – it remains the only season in which Carlisle have
met them on level terms, so to speak.

The Carlisle team that travelled to Highbury for the return League
game had a slightly unfamiliar look to it. Peter Carr was suspended and
so Bobby Parker moved across to play right-back. Chris Balderstone was
drafted in as sweeper, the position he had often occupied the previous
campaign, and Eddie Spearritt came in at left-back in place of the injured
John Gorman. It was not Spearritt's most natural position but it was a
chance for him to play first-team football and perhaps stake his claim to
a more regular place. It was a challenge that he was pleased to accept.

Carlisle's only previous visit to Highbury was for the FA Cup-tie in
January 1951 that attracted an attendance of 57,932. Twenty-four years
later the gate was a more modest 21,000. The Gunners were only two
places above Carlisle and might have been suffering from the effects of a
hard midweek Cup replay. Second Division York had drawn at Highbury
the previous Saturday and it took the Gunners extra-time in the replay
before they came through.

It was the proverbial game of two halves with Carlisle dominating the
first and Arsenal the second. With the score at 1-1 and just seconds
remaining, Arsenal were awarded a corner and George Armstrong's kick
was flicked on by Brian Kidd. I can remember standing on the terracing
behind the Carlisle goal and following what looked to me like a loose
scrum on the goal-line. Alex Cropley forced the ball in for the home side.
For the third League game in a row, United had been sunk by a goal in
virtually the last minute. After the game, even Denis Compton was
moved to remark that Carlisle were too good to go down but the refrain
was starting to feel a little hollow.

Elsewhere in the First Division, Ipswich Town were by now back on
top and they were the next visitors to Brunton Park. For Ipswich old boys
Eddie Spearritt and Frank Clarke, they were looking forward to putting
one over on their old club. 'There won't be any old pals act here,' promised Clarke. 'We are desperate for points and although Ipswich are top of
the league I think we will do well.' The centre of attention for many,
though, was a rare appearance by Kevin Beattie on his home turf. Having
said that, he had made an unexpected return to Carlisle only three weeks
earlier. While travelling to an England Under-23 match at Aberdeen, he

decided to go home to Carlisle instead, complaining he could not cope with the pressure of being a top footballer. The next day, Beattie returned to Ipswich and for a while it looked as if his international career might end almost before it had begun. The affair took place soon after Don Revie had taken over as England manager but common sense prevailed and Beattie was reprieved.

Bobby Robson was the Ipswich boss and before the game he was seen at the Sheepmount playing fields, observing an Under-15 match between Cumberland Schools and Greater Manchester Schools. He was accompanied by John Carruthers, the Ipswich scout based in Carlisle who had discovered not just Kevin Beattie but also David Geddis and Robin Turner, who had also made their way down to Suffolk. Whether or not Robson found any more footballing talent that Saturday morning is not recorded but over the years the Carlisle area had proved to be a rich seam of footballing talent for Bobby Robson's Ipswich.

As for the match at Brunton Park, Kevin Beattie was made Ipswich captain for the occasion. Ironically, he was the only Carlisle-born player on either side. For Carlisle, Eddie Spearritt made his home debut at right-back, while John Gorman and Dennis Martin returned to the fray. The game itself proved to be one of the most entertaining of the season at Brunton Park. Frank Clarke duly notched a goal against his old club and Joe Laidlaw also found the net. In between, Trevor Whymark headed home for the visitors, while Carlisle also missed a twice-taken penalty. First Bobby Parker had his shot saved and when the kick was ordered to be retaken, Les O'Neill hit it hard, high and wide. For once, however, Carlisle held on through that crucial 90th minute to record a famous and vital victory.

Three days later Beattie's rehabilitation with the national team was confirmed when he appeared for England Under-23s against Wales at Wrexham. Nor was his the only Carlisle connection in this match. For some time there had been speculation that United's elevation to the top flight could give some of the players more chance of gaining international recognition. Scotland had seemed the likeliest of the home countries to benefit and Willie Ormond, the Scottish team manager, had paid a visit to Brunton Park when Chelsea were the visitors. Part of his brief had been to check on the form of John Gorman and Dennis Martin, though sadly neither of them was to win the international cap many felt they deserved.

It was, however, Mick Barry who was about to gain a measure of international recognition and realise his ambition to represent the land of his father. 'All my life it has been Wales, Wales, Wales,' was his reaction when he learned he had been selected to play against England. 'Even if I had the option of playing for England, I would have opted for the Welsh shirt.' With half an hour to go, Barry came on to replace the injured Leighton James and so gain his precious Welsh cap. It was a proud moment for Barry and his family and also some acknowledgement for his club of the quality of football they were capable of producing. For the record, it may be noted that England Under-23s won the game 2-0 with Kevin Beattie scoring England's first goal. In goal for England was Mervyn Day who many years later was to both play for and manage Carlisle United.

The victory over Ipswich had given a much-needed boost to Carlisle's hopes of staying in the top flight. Even though they remained third from bottom, United were now just three points from safety. For now, however, it was the turn of the FA Cup to command the club's attention as the Cumbrians faced the prospect of a home game against Alan Ashman's old club West Brom. The Baggies had come through the third round by emphatically defeating Bolton after a replay. 'Of course the Cup is important to us,' Ashman averred when discussing the forthcoming tie. 'There is a lot at stake both cash wise and prestige wise. A long cup run means a lot of cash for a club like Carlisle United. It can bring in much needed cash that could come in handy for Division One survival.'

Despite his two-match suspension coming to an end, Peter Carr did not immediately regain the full-back berth that Eddie Spearritt retained for this game. The team, in fact, was unchanged from that which had defeated Ipswich. This gave Dennis Martin the chance to play against his former club. The game was almost called off due to heavy rain earlier in the week but the pitch was passed as playable and the healthy crowd of almost 15,000 included a sizeable contingent from the West Midlands.

Despite the conditions, it proved to be another entertaining encounter for the spectators. Frank Clarke and Joe Laidlaw scored for the second week running, while Bobby Owen also weighed in with the crucial third goal. For the visitors, Tony Brown with a penalty and Gordon Nisbet kept the game alive almost to the end but Carlisle held on to record their first back-to-back victories since the start of the campaign. 'That was a satisfying result for us as a team,' was the verdict of Dennis Martin after the game. 'The draw against Mansfield isn't too bad although we will have to treat them with respect. Personally I suppose beating West Brom brought a lot of pleasure to me because they were my former club but it is always nice to win, no matter who the opposition are.'

The victory over West Bromwich put Carlisle into the fifth round for only the fourth and, to date, last time in their history. At that stage of the season, however, the priority had to be securing the club's First Division status for another year. This entailed trying to put some daylight between Carlisle and the two sides, Leicester and Luton, who were below them in the League, as well as bridging the gap with the next batch of clubs three or four points ahead – Birmingham and the London trio of Arsenal, Chelsea and Spurs. Carlisle's next opponents were West Ham, and for this match Carlisle were again able to field an unchanged side.

The game was played on a heavy and muddy Upton Park pitch and the Hammers came through 2-0. Trevor Brooking was again outstanding in the heavy conditions and Carlisle were never able to fully counter his influence. One who did his best, though, was Ray Train who enjoyed a rare bout of national attention through the televising of this fixture. The game was featured on *Match of the Day* and as part of the analysis, Jimmy Hill chose to highlight the contribution of Ray Train. Ray was one of the quietest men at the club, one of his main claims to fame being that his size four boots were reputedly the smallest of any player in the Football League. He tended, if anything, to avoid publicity rather than court it, preferring to let his performances on the park do the talking. Signed originally as a forward from Walsall, his only previous club, his favoured role was that of an engine-room midfielder alongside Les O'Neill, another player whose lack of inches belied his effectiveness.

The match at Upton Park had been in doubt due to the heavy conditions but it later transpired that the West Ham players had been keen to play. Knowing Carlisle's reputation for the 'push and run' style of play, they felt they would have a better chance against the Cumbrians on a heavy and difficult playing surface. Although it was a slightly backhanded compliment, it did indicate that other clubs such as West Ham admired Carlisle's style of football. Les Cocker, who was Don Revie's assistant with both Leeds and England, was also at the game and he offered another perspective on Carlisle's struggle to survive in the top flight: 'On a pitch like that I thought Carlisle did very well. They could have had a couple of goals but the ball stuck awkwardly for their forwards. The difficulty for them is that they always go for the whole loaf. At Leeds we would go away and know for some matches we could not go for the whole loaf and therefore set out to win half the loaf, i.e. draw rather than a win. Carlisle cannot do that. They do not have the players for a lengthy containing job. They must go for a win every time but today West Ham were in the groove.'

Seven days later it was the turn of Sheffield United to make the journey to Brunton Park. By now, Peter Carr was back in the team but left-back John Gorman had been suffering from an abdominal injury and the decision was taken to rest him. In attack, Hughie McIlmoyle, who had scarcely featured for the club since Christmas, returned to the bench. The Blades were lying in mid-table, almost safe from relegation but too far adrift to be title challengers. Their side included Garry Jones, on loan from Bolton, who was making his debut. In front of a crowd of 12,023, the lowest of the season, it was Jones who scored the only goal of the game midway through the first half, capitalising on slack defending. It was one of the few chances the visitors created but, despite dominating possession, Carlisle failed to rise to the occasion.

At least Carlisle still had the FA Cup-tie at Mansfield to occupy their minds for the next few days. 'We're putting all the worries of the league to the back of our minds this week and we'll be concentrating on getting to the Sixth Round of the Cup,' Alan Ashman confirmed. 'We're going to forget about Saturday's result and our position in the league for this week at least. Instead we'll all be working on a winning formula for Saturday's cup clash with Mansfield. That is all that matters.' At least Carlisle had relatively few injury worries, the main exception being the luckless Eddie Prudham, whose leg was back in plaster for a further two weeks.

Although Mansfield Town were the last survivors from the Fourth Division, the FA Cup that year had seen a series of impressive performances from non-league teams and the Stags may well have felt it was their year to progress even further. Wimbledon were a Southern League side in those days, but they had won 1-0 at First Division Burnley. In the fourth round they had astounded the nation by drawing 0-0 at Leeds before unluckily going out in the replay – at Selhurst Park – to a deflected own-goal. Leatherhead of the Isthmian League defeated two Football League sides before losing 2-3 to First Division Leicester. Altrincham and Wycombe Wanderers meanwhile held Everton and Middlesbrough respectively before their illustrious opponents came through unconvincingly when the replays were held. Nor were cup shocks confined to the FA Cup. Fourth Division Chester overcame two First Division clubs, including Leeds, in the League Cup before narrowly losing in the semifinals to Aston Villa.

As for Mansfield themselves, they had the best record in the Football League at the time. They were racing away with the Fourth Division title, having lost just two of their 29 League games all season. They were unbeaten in eighteen League and cup matches stretching back to the end of October and their confidence level understandably was sky high. Dave Smith was the Stags' boss and he had already picked up two Manager of the Month awards during the campaign. Before coming to Mansfield, he had been the reserve-team manager at Arsenal and had compiled a dossier on Carlisle when United played the Gunners in the FA Cup two years previously. The game at Mansfield's Field Mill ground was made all-ticket with a crowd limit of 22,000. Carlisle took their allocation of 5,000 and the expectation was that the encounter would be a sell out. United even chartered the 'League Liner' train to transport some 450 fans by rail to the game.

The game was to be televised on *Match of the Day* but this too seemed to be a less than auspicious omen. The opening day of the campaign had seen United win at Chelsea on *Match of the Day* on the BBC. Since then Carlisle had lost to Liverpool and West Ham in later appearances on the programme. ITV had broadcast away games against Newcastle, Sheffield United, Wolves, Coventry and Luton, and Carlisle had been defeated in all these matches. As a result, Carlisle's record was 'played 8; lost 7' as far as television was concerned. The approach of ITV to Carlisle's achievement in reaching the First Division also seemed somewhat lukewarm. Kenneth Wolstenholme, now of Tyne Tees TV, had promised that the company would focus on the big three North East clubs and Carlisle, but there had been virtually no evidence of this as far as the Cumbrians were concerned. Meanwhile, Granada TV seemed reluctant to send a camera crew up to Carlisle, which was also way outside their area, while Border TV did not seem to be capable of mounting a successful televising operation from Brunton Park.

It was little wonder, therefore, that many pundits saw the game as a giant-killing probability, with Mansfield brushing aside a Carlisle team who were only in the top flight by a fluke. Brian Clough, for one, was confident of a victory for the Stags by a 3-1 margin. Speaking on TV at lunchtime he fingered Eddie Spearritt as the weak link in the Carlisle team. Since he and Spearritt had had a major falling out while both were at Brighton, it was a judgment that smacked more of the need to settle a score rather than a balanced assessment of the game in prospect.

The attendance at the game was not quite capacity but still a very respectable 18,293. It was Mansfield's best for six years and one that has not been subsequently exceeded. The Stags ran out and milked the applause of the crowd before the start, while manager Dave Smith let it be known that the champagne was on ice ready for the celebrations afterwards. Unfortunately for the home fans, the game did not quite turn out as they had hoped. After soaking up early pressure, Bobby Owen's goal on the turn after nineteen minutes rocked the Stags. Despite periods of heavy pressure, Carlisle held on to claim victory and put the club in the quarter-finals for the first time ever. Allan Ross in goal and Bill Green were outstanding, but the whole team, not least the unfairly maligned Eddie Spearritt, played their part in the triumph.

After re-enacting for the camera the goal-line clearance that he had made at one point to keep Carlisle in the Cup, captain Bill Green gave his verdict on the match: 'We approached the tie in the right way and out on the field we worked and tackled and thought and ran. I don't think we have worked harder this season. As captain I was elated by the way we won the match. Mansfield were very, very good. They played the way you would expect of a Fourth Division side taking on a Division One team and the great thing for us was we responded to the fight. I don't feel any-thing but pride in the whole team.' Allan Ross gave his own shorter assessment when he commented that Carlisle won because they played Mansfield at their own game and turned themselves into a Fourth Division team for a day. He also revealed that Dave Smith's cockiness had rebounded on him in terms of Carlisle's own approach to the match. Carlisle's reward for their win was a home tie against Second Division Fulham, but first of all the need to secure vital League points had again to be the top priority.

CHAPTER 8

1974-75: The Dream is Over

The win at Mansfield may have been an important result, but by the Monday morning the club was faced again with the reality of a battle against relegation. 'Whatever I say will not stop the lads from thinking about the cup,' Alan Ashman realistically conceded, 'but we know what our priorities are: league points. We need them badly and this is what we will be concentrating on till March.'

The club was now faced with four consecutive Saturday home fixtures, including the FA Cup-tie against Fulham. Two of the other games were against fellow strugglers Leicester City and Luton Town, where anything less than maximum points was for Carlisle unthinkable. First up at Brunton Park, however, were Queens Park Rangers and their ex-Carlisle star Stan Bowles.

Rangers, like Sheffield United a fortnight earlier, were comfortably placed in mid-table, though rather ominously they had one of the best away records in the division. Stan Bowles was in the Rangers line-up and was given a generous round of applause when he appeared. For once, he did not score against his old club, although his dive when put through in a one-on-one against Allan Ross was clearly designed to win a penalty. Carlisle kept the same eleven as had won at Mansfield, and after Givens had put the visitors ahead, Bobby Owen – with his first goal since Boxing Day – headed in for the equaliser. Not for the first time, Carlisle dominated possession without being able to convert chances into goals, and eventually Givens scored again in the second half from a weak defensive clearance. Yet again, a team that Carlisle should have at least held at home had gone away with both points.

Three days after the QPR match, Carlisle travelled to Elland Road for their first ever visit. Leeds were the current League champions but had fatally handicapped their defence of the title by the disastrous appointment of Brian Clough as their manager for 44 days. Clough's replacement was Jimmy Armfield, and under his thoughtful guidance Leeds too had reached the FA Cup quarter-finals and the same stage of the European Cup. Even the retention of the League title no longer seemed impossible in what was proving to be an unusually close contest. Stoke City had just displaced Everton at the top, but only a handful of points separated the leading clubs. Derby County for instance were lying seventh but only three points behind the leaders.

Carlisle took an unchanged team to Leeds, who themselves made just one change from the side that had won at Middlesbrough three days earlier – with Eddie Gray back in for Terry Cooper. This meant that Frank Clarke would be in opposition to younger brother Allan, who had scored the only goal at the match at Boro.

Allan Clarke scored again in the match against Carlisle, which the home side won 3-1. 'Leeds cut us to ribbons in the second half,' Allan Ross admitted afterwards. Too many of Carlisle's defeats had come about when they looked the better side until they reached their opponents' penalty area. The only bright spot on the night came from Joe Laidlaw's fine individual goal but unfortunately Carlisle were three down by that point and it was little more than a consolation effort. On the night, Laidlaw had been one of the few Carlisle players who had looked the part, along with perhaps Bill Green and the ever reliable Ray Train. What was certainly not in doubt was which of the Clarke brothers was the happier as they left the field together.

The defeat at Elland Road made it look even more likely that Carlisle United would be playing Second Division football next season. That prospect in itself was sufficient to concentrate the minds of the board and the bank manager. The club had budgeted to earn about £7,500 from each home game in Division One and some £2,000 from each away game, this being the era when clubs shared their gate receipts. Over a 21-game season this would amount to almost £200,000. Life in Division Two was expected to yield £4,000 for each home game and £1,000 for every match away from Brunton Park. Over the season this would total a mere £105,000, i.e. a shortfall of almost £100,000 compared to life in Division One. There would clearly be some savings, with smaller crowds leading to a limited saving on expenses, but it was a minuscule amount by comparison. Alan Ashman pledged that the club would buy if need be to preserve its First Division status but as ever it was clear that this would only be if the price was right.

One approach that the club was able to resist was a request from Workington to take Hugh McIlmoyle on loan until the end of the season. Apart from one appearance coming off the bench, the Scot had not been a member of the first team since the Boxing Day clash with Newcastle, but he was still regarded as an integral member of the squad. He provided a vital cover role and, even though now aged 35, was still a class player. As for Cumbria's only other League club, it had again been a difficult season, with Workington occupying a bottom-four spot for almost the entire campaign. Crowds remained low, even though the two Cumbrian sides alternated their home fixture dates. In October, manager George

Aitken resigned and Colin Meldrum was appointed. Amazingly, he won the Fourth Division Manager of the Month award for January after the Reds went nine games unbeaten. Sadly, this prompted a succession of defeats and Meldrum himself left the club in April. There was, though, a happy ending of sorts as once again Workington survived their re-election battle.

The weekend following the Elland Road defeat it was the turn of Leicester City to play at Brunton Park. The Foxes had just endured a disastrous run of fourteen games without a win that had seen them plunge from the safety of mid-table to bottom of the table and likely relegation candidates. That run had finally ended the week before with a 3-0 victory over Tottenham. As Luton Town had drawn with Stoke City on the same day, the defeat by QPR had finally pushed Carlisle down to the bottom of the League. It had, though, been a difficult season for Leicester City. Peter Shilton had been in a contractual dispute with the club and had been transferred to Stoke City; rather like Gordon Banks seven years earlier when Shilton had arrived to challenge his first-team place. Keith Weller also proved a difficult person to handle, having refused to play in the second half of one match, though he later settled his differences with the club.

The Leicester City game was to follow the pattern that was becoming all too familiar. Carlisle again fielded an unchanged team, though after his recent injury problems it was John Gorman who occupied the substitutes bench. Frank Worthington was probably the most celebrated name in the Foxes' rank, a gifted player in the Stan Bowles mould who should have won more than eight caps for England. His League career with eleven different clubs totalled 757 appearances and lasted over twenty years and he scored at least once in each of 21 consecutive campaigns. True to form, it was his dipping shot midway through the second half that produced the only goal in the game at Brunton Park and condemned Carlisle to another home defeat.

There was, however, still the prospect of a first ever appearance in the quarter-finals for Carlisle United. Fulham were lying just below halfway in the Second Division table when they travelled to Brunton Park for the game but they were not a side to be underestimated. In Bobby Moore and Alan Mullery they had two players of the highest class and though both were well past 30 they were still formidable opponents. Alec Stock, the Cottagers' manager, had just been named Second Division Manager of the Month. Fulham had been unbeaten in the League in February as well as causing the upset of the fifth round by winning at Everton. As well as the experience of Moore and Mullery, Fulham had three front players in

Busby, Barrett and Jimmy Conway (the father of future Carlisle player Paul Conway) who had pace and could break quickly out of defence. It was this tactic and two goals from Busby that had caused the downfall of Everton.

The game had, like the League fixture with Newcastle, been made all-ticket with a crowd limit of 28,000. Fulham took their full allocation and over 5,000 of their fans made the long journey north, where they occupied the scratching pen side of the ground. Yet despite reaching the quarter-finals, Carlisle's Cup run was much less lucrative than in the previous season when they had lost to Liverpool in the fourth round. With two replays, nearly 115,000 fans had seen those four games compared with only 74,000 spectators who would watch the four games in the 1974-75 season. Although the tie did not quite sell out, Fulham could take some satisfaction in contributing to a final attendance of 21,570. This proved to be Carlisle's best gate of the whole season, a remarkable statistic in some ways as it meant Fulham attracted a bigger crowd than more obvious suspects such as Newcastle, Leeds, Liverpool and Tottenham.

For this tie, John Gorman returned to left-back in place of Eddie Spearritt. Chris Balderstone took the place of the injured Frank Clarke while the whole team was said to be on a bonus of £60 a man to reach the semi-finals. The Fulham team was almost the same as had won at Everton, which meant that Bobby Moore was making his first appearance at Brunton Park. For Bobby Parker in particular it was the chance to come up against the player upon whom he had modelled his own style of play. Meanwhile, the ITV cameras were in attendance at the ground for the first time this season as the two television networks divided up the four ties between them.

The game proved to be a tale of two goalkeepers. Peter Mellor had gifted Carlisle one of their goals with a fumbled save on Fulham's last visit in October 1973. How Carlisle could have done with a repeat performance. Instead Mellor chose to have the game of his life, at different times making brilliant saves from a Bill Green header, a Les O'Neill volley and shots from Messrs Laidlaw and Owen. Meanwhile, Allan Ross at the other end was almost a spectator for much of the match and there was even a theory that this comparative inactivity contributed to what eventually happened. Midway through the second half a harmless looking cross from Viv Busby was unaccountably missed by both Rossie and full-back Peter Carr. Les Barrett was left to tap the ball into an empty net for probably the easiest goal of his whole career, while for poor Allan Ross it was undoubtedly the worst moment of his fifteen years at Brunton Park. The fact that but for his brilliance on the day, Carlisle would have struggled to get past Preston and Mansfield in earlier rounds was very little consolation.

'Crucifying' was Alan Ashman's verdict on the defeat and even now it ranks as one of the most disappointing results in the club's history. If ever Carlisle were going to reach an FA Cup final, it was in that season. As it was, Fulham went on to defeat Birmingham City in the semi-finals before losing an all-London final to West Ham in which Peter Mellor was at fault for one of the Hammers' two goals. Carlisle, however, were left to pick up the pieces. 'In our present situation at the bottom of the table with the disappointment of losing such a vital cup tie you don't lose your nerve,' Ashman commented. 'You don't panic all over the place. There is no question of accepting we are going to be a Second Division side. I am on record before the Fulham match as saying that retaining our First Division status is more important than winning the FA Cup. We still have everything to play for.'

It was little wonder, though, that the next game against Luton should attract a mere 8,339 spectators. It was the lowest Division One gate anywhere all season. Hughie McIlmoyle made a surprise reappearance in the side, coming in for the injured Frank Clarke, and John Gorman replaced Eddie Spearritt. With only one win in the past eight games, Luton's recent record had scarcely been any better than Carlisle's and it was little wonder that there was a distinct lack of atmosphere on the day. Given the disappointments of the past month, this was no surprise.

With the 90 minutes almost expired and the score 1-1, Luton's Ron Futcher hit a hopeful centre towards the Carlisle goal. Either the strong wind caught the ball or Allan Ross in goal misjudged it, or both, but somehow it wafted its way into the corner of the net. If the defeat of Tottenham was the zenith of Carlisle's season, this was surely the nadir as the team trooped off with the abuse of the crowd – or at least those who had not already left – ringing in their ears. It was also a sad way for Hughie McIlmoyle to make his final appearance in a Carlisle shirt. The popular Scot deserved a better curtain call.

The defeat by Luton was generally regarded as cementing Carlisle's return to the Second Division. Peter Carr at least was prepared to be positive about the situation. 'If we start pushing the ball around like we did at the beginning of the season, we can think about returning to Division One at the first attempt. When we went to the top of Division One we were a good side and deserved to be there.' He also, though, recognised that things had changed. 'Now nobody seems to be wanting the ball. They are frightened of being in possession. The confidence we had earlier is gone.' The truth was that the sequence of four home defeats on four successive Saturdays had been too much for many fans. Some of the team were actually finding it easier to play away from Brunton Park.

Four days later the theory was put to the test against Manchester City at Maine Road. City no longer looked like title contenders but were still placed above halfway in the table. Frank Clarke returned to the Carlisle line-up, as did Eddie Spearritt for John Gorman, who was rested. Before the game Alan Ashman decided upon a novel tactic. Instead of giving the team their usual pep talk, he and Dick Young left the dressing room ten minutes before the start of the game to let the players ponder their situation and motivate themselves. Whether it was this initiative or some light relief coursing through the team – now that they knew that the relegation battle was almost certainly lost – it worked. Joe Laidlaw's brace included a superb twenty- yard volley over keeper Joe Corrigan who had edged just a yard too far off his line as United pulled off a surprise 2-1 victory, all the goals coming before half-time.

The following Saturday, Carlisle travelled to the Victoria Ground at Stoke for the first time ever. The Potters still harboured their own hopes of a title win. Despite losing at home to Ipswich in midweek, they were still just four points behind leaders Everton. Carlisle kept the same side that had pulled off the win at Maine Road and at half-time were holding the home side to a goal apiece. The final score of 5-2 to the home side was rather more conclusive, with Terry Conroy becoming the only player to score a hat-trick against the Cumbrians in the whole season. It was Carlisle's heaviest defeat since the 1-6 reverse at Luton at the start of the previous season.

'Stoke City were for my money the only team that really trounced us,' Allan Ross later admitted. 'Both home and away they taught us a lesson.' It was a heavy defeat and also the biggest win all season for the home side. Whereas at Carlisle it had been Alan Hudson who had dominated the proceedings, this time the star man for the Potters was fellow midfielder Geoff Salmons. His long passes set up two of the Stoke goals, while he scored the last himself with a 25-yard strike. That made the score 5-1 but United were not quite dead and buried as Peter Carr netted his first ever goal for Carlisle to add a bit of respectability to the final result. That he should score against Peter Shilton, the most expensive goalkeeper in the world, was an added bonus for the young defender. Nor was this Carlisle's only consolation from their defeat. As they emerged from their dressing room after the game, a group of Stoke fans, who had stayed behind, greeted them to let them know that Carlisle were the best team to come to Stoke that season and that the club did not deserve to be relegated. While it was getting rather late to think about escaping the drop, it was more evidence that Carlisle were at least respected for their style of football.

Three days later Carlisle set off to Birmingham's St Andrews ground for their third away match in a week. Although they had been in no real danger of relegation, Birmingham had spent virtually the entire season in the lower half of the table. Trevor Francis was their star player but he had just returned from a four-month lay off through injury. The game proved to be one of the most unpleasant Carlisle were involved in all season, due in part to some lenient refereeing. A bad foul on Ray Train set the scene after just three minutes. Birmingham keeper Gary Sprake was stretchered off, although he was later able to return, but Bobby Owen was not so lucky when his shin was gashed and he too left the field before half-time. It was inevitably Trevor Francis who provided one of the few moments of quality in the match when he scored from 30 yards. United seldom looked likely to equalise, though Kenny Burns' second goal which clinched the match came just four minutes from the end.

By the time Carlisle played their next game, on Easter Saturday, their League position was looking almost hopeless. After their victory at Brunton Park, Luton had gone on to win their next two games to lift them five points clear of Carlisle. Tottenham, too, had won on Good Friday and they too had a five-point lead over United, which in the days of two points for a win meant two wins and a draw just to catch up. As Carlisle now had only six games left to play, survival was becoming something of a tall order. The next visitors to Brunton Park moreover were scheduled to be Everton who had been top of Division One for most of the past two months. Against that, Carlisle were the only team to win at Goodison Park in the League all season. Moreover, the last leaders to arrive at Brunton Park had been Ipswich in mid-January and by the end of the match they were top no longer.

Everton had maintained their place at the top despite in some ways a relatively modest record. They had been in the top six all season yet had won only five more matches at the time than had Carlisle. The difference was in the Merseysiders' ability to avoid defeat. As well as only one reverse at home, they had lost just four times away from Goodison and both statistics were the best in Division One. The Toffees were also draw specialists and no fewer than sixteen of their games had finished all square. Nevertheless, they were the famous Everton FC and top of the League as thousands of their fans journeyed north on Easter Saturday. The crowd at Brunton Park was swollen by their presence to over 16,000, easily the best League gate since the visit of Newcastle on Boxing Day. It was, moreover, seven years since Everton had last played at Brunton

Park. That had been a fourth round FA Cup-tie which the Toffees, boasting the famous half-back line of Harvey, Ball and Kendall, had won far more convincingly than the 2-0 scoreline would suggest. In fact, in my own memory that Everton team was as good a side as I have ever seen here at Brunton Park.

History, though, was not about to repeat itself; in fact far from it. For this game Allan Ross in goal was rested and Tom Clarke came in for his first match in over four months. John Gorman returned at full-back and Chris Balderstone replaced the injured Bobby Owen. Meanwhile, the presence of Everton had persuaded Granada to travel up to provide TV highlights. The first half remained goalless with the League leaders apparently content to retain the point they started out with, rather than try to win against the bottom club.

The tactic came unstuck in the second half when United were awarded a penalty. Joe Laidlaw had recently become the nominated penalty taker, after the problems his teammates had found with spot-kicks. There was nothing too sophisticated about his approach. 'I will decide the area I am putting it in and then thump the ball hard. The harder you hit it the less chance the keeper has. That is my attitude.'

It certainly worked against Everton, despite Laidlaw having to retake the kick when Frank Clarke stepped into the 'D' before the kick was taken. A superb Dennis Martin chip, thankfully recorded for posterity by the cameras, brought a second goal from Peter Carr's free-kick before Frank Clarke added a third. To compound Everton's misery, Liverpool won to displace them at the top of the table.

The victory over Everton at least gave Carlisle the honour of completing one 'double' and four days later they entertained Burnley. They too had title aspirations and had been second in the League as late as mid-March. Nowadays, it is taken for granted that almost any competitive football match will be recorded on tape but back in 1975 this was far from being the case. Less than half United's First Division matches had TV cameras present, especially those at Brunton Park, but if ever a game from that season deserved to be recorded for posterity, it was this one. United won 4-2 thanks to two late goals, including a superb 25-yarder from Ray Train, which earned Carlisle both points after Burnley had fought back from being two goals down. Joe Laidlaw weighed in with two strikes, including another powerful spot-kick, and Les O'Neill grabbed another of his trademark goals, bursting through from midfield. Burnley too played their part in this classic encounter, their outstanding player being Peter Noble, who had so nearly joined Carlisle United two years earlier.

Their defeat ended any lingering hopes Burnley might have had of winning the title but still left Carlisle bottom of the table. Although there was no real chance of avoiding the drop, at least the club was going down fighting.

Not since the defeat of Spurs had Carlisle won back-to-back League games. The prospect of another home fixture the next Saturday against Coventry City held out the realistic prospect of a third successive victory. For this game, Bobby Owen returned to replace the injured Les O'Neill, while Eddie Prudham was fit enough to return to the bench for his first appearance since December. The crowd meanwhile had dropped down to less than 11,000. Perhaps those who chose not to attend knew the score in advance as the two sides played out a goalless draw. The point suited Coventry who had an outside chance of being sucked into the relegation battle. It also enabled Carlisle to briefly climb back above Luton and up to second from bottom. The main casualty was Frank Clarke who went off injured but at least it gave Eddie Prudham his chance. He managed an hour's football without ill-effects. Elsewhere, Fulham were doing battle with Birmingham City in their FA Cup semi-final at Hillsborough, where a gate of 55,000 watched a 1-1 draw. What would United have given to be a part of that game?

Four days later Fulham won the replay 1-0 at Maine Road and the chance to play West Ham in an all-London final after the Hammers had defeated Ipswich, also after a replay. Elsewhere that same evening, Derby County defeated Wolves by a solitary goal to become the seventh side that season to top the League in one of the tightest title races for years. Carlisle's plight, however, was becoming desperate, despite the revival in their form. They now needed at least a draw just to be certain of avoiding relegation and were faced with a trip to Anfield where Liverpool had their own championship ambitions.

Tom Clarke retained his place between the posts for this match. He for one was looking forward to playing in front of the Kop and not just because the day happened to be his birthday. He had been at Brunton Park since joining from Airdrie in 1970 but the form of Allan Ross throughout that period meant that his fellow Scot had only limited opportunities to feature in the first team. The nine appearances he made in the First Division was actually his best season's total while at Brunton Park. The Everton game had not asked too many questions of Carlisle's defence but that could pose its own problems. 'Most of the action was centred on the Everton goal and I was out of the game for long spells,' he later recalled. 'It is the hardest thing for a goalkeeper to stand virtually as a spectator for most of the game then suddenly be asked to produce the goods.' He had been blameless for Burnley's two goals, while the hardest save he had to make in the Coventry game was to rescue a misplaced back-pass from John Gorman. Now he and the rest of the United team were set to appear before the famous Anfield Kop in front of probably the biggest crowd they would see all season.

The attendance at Liverpool was 46,073, which as well as being the best crowd to watch Carlisle during that season is also the highest League gate ever for any Carlisle match. The game itself was some way short of a classic. Les O'Neill was able to return after missing the Coventry game, and Frank Clarke was in the starting line up. As usual Carlisle played neat attractive football, but without creating many chances, yet were worth going in all-square at half-time. Early in the second period, Frank Clarke's departure through injury seemed to upset the United rhythm and Toshack headed in a Phil Neal corner soon afterwards. A quarter of an hour before the end a scrappy goal from Kevin Keegan sealed Carlisle's fate as they were officially relegated back to Division Two. Elsewhere, Derby beat West Ham 1-0 to remain in first place.

The final home game of the season took place a week later against Wolves. The Molyneux club had, like Midland neighbours Coventry and Birmingham, enjoyed a season spent largely in mid-table. They had, however, recorded the highest score of the campaign when they thrashed Chelsea 7-1 and more recently had put five goals past Luton Town. In a changed line up, the two Eddies, Prudham and Spearritt, were recalled to the side, as was keeper Allan Ross. It had been a difficult few weeks for Rossie, in particular following the Fulham debacle, and with his health beginning to suffer, he had been rested for a while. Now he felt able to return to his accustomed position between the posts. The game attracted an attendance of 9,707, which apart from the match against Luton was the lowest crowd of the season at Brunton Park. In fact, they were the only sub-10,000 gates anywhere during the whole of the Division One campaign. At least the home fans were rewarded with a win, the twelfth and last of the season. It was Dennis Martin who scored what proved to be United's 43rd and final goal in Division One, hitting home from eight yards after Les O'Neill's shot had been blocked. In truth, however, the game had an end of season air about it, with only pride being at stake for either side.

Elsewhere, Derby had drawn 0-0 at Leicester, but their Merseyside rivals Liverpool and Everton had both lost. These results put Derby very much in the driving seat for the League championship, as neither of the Merseyside duo could now catch the Rams. The chances were that they would need just one point from their final match at home to Carlisle.

Even that scenario would only come about if Ipswich Town, the only club who could now halt the Rams, defeated Manchester City in their midweek encounter at Maine Road. Derby had timed their surge to the summit with perfection, winning six of their last eight games and drawing the other two. They may not have reached top spot until the second week in April but once there, they were not willing to relinquish it without a fight. After the traumas of the reign and the subsequent acrimonious departure of Brian Clough, Derby manager Dave Mackay could be pleased with the way his team had responded to the challenge.

While not taking sides, many at Brunton Park were hoping that Ipswich would do the necessary to ensure that the title was still at stake when Carlisle travelled to the Baseball Ground. It was also a last chance to show that despite finishing bottom of the table, Carlisle were not so bad a team. 'We want to wind up the season on a winning note and what better way to do it than by beating the team who could well be champions,' Bill Green remarked when viewing the prospects for the match at Derby. 'It's going to be a top of the table v bottom clash and we will show that there is just a hairline between success and failure. We are not the worst team in Division One. We have learned a lot in the top flight and unfortunately too late to save us from being relegated. That is why a win on Saturday will be so important.'

In the event, Ipswich failed to do the necessary and despite Brian Hamilton's second-half equaliser, Town were unable to secure the two points necessary to deny Derby the championship. History therefore repeated itself as for the second time in four seasons, the Rams clinched the title without playing a game, as all their rivals faltered at the last hurdle. Four years earlier the Derby squad was already on an end of season Mediterranean break. This time they still had their own League programme to complete on the notoriously muddy Baseball Ground surface. Eddie Spearritt for one was unfazed by the prospect, having scored there while with Ipswich Town but all the Carlisle team were determined to end their First Division campaign on a high note.

First of all though, there were the pleasantries to be observed. The gates had been locked on a 38,000 crowd long before the kick-off as Carlisle, in a role reversal of the opening day at Stamford Bridge, sportingly applauded the Derby team onto the pitch to receive the League trophy. Among the watching celebrities were Willie Carlin, the ex-Carlisle midfielder, whom Brian Clough had later signed from Sheffield United, and Tim Ward, the ex-Carlisle boss who more relevantly had been both player and manager at the Baseball Ground. As for the game itself, Frank Clarke was fit to return to the Carlisle line up in place of Eddie Prudham while Derby kept the same team that had gained that vital draw at Leicester seven days earlier.

Played in bright sunshine, the game itself lacked the urgency that would certainly have been present had there been more than pride riding upon the result. 'Carlisle fail to shake up sleepy Rams,' was the judgment of the local Derby newspaper as neither side was able to create many clear-cut chances. Perhaps a draw was a reasonable outcome. The home side had avoided what would have been an embarrassing loss against the bottom club and one, moreover, that had already defeated them 3-0 at Brunton Park. Carlisle United meanwhile had the satisfaction of being unbeaten in both matches against the League champions. Not only that, they were the only club apart from Everton to deny Derby a goal in 180 minutes of football. As Carlisle took their leave of the top flight, it was not that bad an epitaph to take back with them to Division Two.

CHAPTER 9

Gone but not Forgotten

As the players left the Baseball Ground on 26 April 1975 knowing that their next game would be in the Second Division, the club's retained list had already been determined. It came as little surprise that Hughie McIlmoyle and Chris Balderstone were to be released. It had been six weeks since Hughie had featured in the line up. Since Christmas he had been rather marginalised and had made only a handful of appearances in the second half of the campaign. The following season saw him return to playing for Morton, back in his hometown of Greenock, before moving south to Leicester, where he spent many years working at the Walkers crisp factory. Taking early retirement, he has now settled in Carlisle and is once again a regular at Brunton Park.

Chris Balderstone's immediate plans on leaving Derby were to take part in a charity cricket match the following day but, at the age of 34, his best days as a footballer were behind him. He was now free to concentrate on his other love of cricket.

Not that Balderstone's soccer career was entirely ended. He had one more season in the Football League, playing for Fourth Division Doncaster Rovers. It was while he was at Belle Vue that he achieved one of his most celebrated feats by playing county cricket and League football in the same day. More specifically, he was 51 not out batting for Leicestershire against Derbyshire at Chesterfield on 15 September 1975, before being driven to Doncaster to play for Rovers in a 1-1 draw against Brentford. The next day he took his score to 116 before being run out. To complete the celebrations, Leicestershire clinched the County Championship for the first time ever while that match was being played.

After his season with Doncaster, he played two seasons for Queen of the South in the Scottish League before ending his soccer days with Enderby Town. His cricket career meanwhile benefited from finally being given first priority and in 1976 he played in two Test matches against the West Indies. When he finally retired after scoring over 19,000 runs and taking some 300 wickets, he joined the panel of umpires. Eventually he moved back to live in Cumbria and was at home when he died suddenly in March 2000 aged 59.

The other players to receive a free transfer were goalkeepers Tom Clarke and Peter MacLachlan, which left Allan Ross as the only keeper on the club's books. Tom Clarke had been five years at Brunton Park since joining the club from Airdrie but he had made only 23 League appearances in that time. With no reserve team and only one substitute allowed at that time, the chances for any second-choice keeper were necessarily limited. He later signed for Preston, for whom he made a single appearance. He now works on the North Sea oilrigs with their regular pattern of 'two weeks on' and 'two weeks off'.

If the chances were limited for a reserve goalkeeper, then the lot of a third choice was even less enviable. One of the few exceptions to this rule came in the 1974 World Cup finals when the Dutch team fielded Jan Jongbloed in goal. He was the only member of the team who was not then playing for Ajax Amsterdam or Feyenoord Rotterdam, apart from Johann Cruyff, formerly of Ajax, who had moved to Barcelona. Jongbloed was always referred to as 'the Dutch third choice goalkeeper', which presumably did little for his confidence, though at least he, and neither of the other choices, was actually in the team.

Peter MacLachlan was a time-served engineer with crane makers Cowan Sheldon and had given up the security of full-time employment to sign as a professional with United in November 1973. He was the only locally born player in the squad, so naturally it was a disappointment to him to be released without ever having made a single League appearance for the club. One of the few consolations he had was to take part in a special mile race run before the 1975 Cup final. Each of the teams in the last sixteen was represented and Peter MacLachlan came in third as he celebrated becoming the first Carlisle United player ever to appear at Wembley. Peter then signed for Morecambe, having been recommended to their manager by Mike Barry and continued to play locally for a number of teams. He was aged 40 when he made his last appearances for Carlisle reserves. He still lives locally and works at the Cumberland Infirmary.

To the rest of the First Division squad fell the task of trying to regain the club's position in the top flight. After all, if Manchester United could bounce back after one season in the Second Division, could not Carlisle United do the same?

Promotion back to Division One was certainly the stated aim of the club and before the new campaign began United were among the bookmakers' favourites to return to the First Division. The team retained a cadre of good young players, including Bill Green, Peter Carr, John Gorman, Bobby Parker, Mike Barry and Ray Train. Their form had attracted the attention of scouts from other clubs and Carlisle had already turned down a bid of £165,000 from Tottenham Hotspur for Bill Green before the season began. For a club with a reputation of buying players at bargain prices and selling them at a profit, the refusal to accept Spurs' cheque was a welcome sign.

On the other hand, the club had been unable to substantially strengthen the squad, with goalkeeper Martin Burleigh being the only new face to appear. He had almost quit the game before reviving his career with Darlington, to whom Carlisle paid £35,000 for his signature. A confident and ebullient character, he would start the season as first-choice keeper, with veteran Allan Ross being relegated to second string. At least Rossie had the consolation of a new two-year contract that suggested that he still had a future at the club he had served for so long.

A reasonably successful pre-season outing in the Texaco Cup was a promising sign of things to come, with wins over both Newcastle and Sunderland. Unfortunately, early season results indicated that the chances of an immediate promotion back to the First Division were not as high as might have been expected. By early September, Carlisle were bottom of Division Two with just one point from five games. Yet apart from goalkeeper Burleigh, the team was the same as had played in the First Division.

Results improved marginally in the next few weeks but it was clear that, for whatever reason, Alan Ashman was having difficulty in motivating most of the players, particularly those who had played regularly in the top flight. On 16 October 1975 he tendered his resignation to the directors. It was a sad way for the man subsequently voted Carlisle's 'Man of the Century' to end his connection with Brunton Park. A few weeks later he became the manager of neighbouring Workington who were, not for the first time, propping up the Fourth Division. Later on he had a spell as boss of Walsall, where he eventually settled. He did some scouting and was assistant manager at Hereford for a while but never again approached the success he had enjoyed at Brunton Park. Alan Ashman died in November 2002 at the age of 74.

Dick Young was once again made caretaker manager, but in a departure from the usual script, was then given the job on a permanent basis. Having once chosen a 23-year-old in Ivor Broadis to be the club's manager, Carlisle United now set a record in the other direction by appointing a 57-year-old to take over the reins at Brunton Park. Moreover though he was obviously steeped in the ways of the club, he had been ill earlier in the season and had as a consequence so far not seen very much of the team's performances on the park. Under Dick Young, results did nevertheless improve, though the team never rose much above mid-table. He was, however, not slow to make changes that he thought were necessary. Allan Ross was restored to the first team in early November, having watched patiently in the stands as United sank down the table. Martin Burleigh had not played at all badly but he was dropped for breaching club discipline, along with Mike Barry. Although Barry was soon back in the team, it was Martin Burleigh who was to spend the remainder of the campaign in the stands, apart from the FA Cup appearance when Rossie was injured.

As well as restoring Allan Ross to the team, Dick Young made another gesture towards the successes of the past in his first signing. George McVitie had been an England Schoolboy international while at school in Carlisle and had then become an apprentice professional at Brunton Park, turning down a host of offers from bigger clubs. An immensely skilful player and a superb crosser of the ball, much of his early tutelage had come from Dick Young. In 1970 Alan Ashman had taken him to West Brom, then three years later George had signed for Oldham. While at Boundary Park his team clinched the Third Division title on the same evening that Carlisle were promoted to Division One. In early December George McVitie returned to Brunton Park in a £12,000 deal and made his debut at Bristol City the same week.

The poor form that the club had shown early in the season was always going to make it hard to sustain a promotion challenge, even though the 1973-74 season had also started in a rather unconvincing manner. The club was certainly unlucky with injuries. Ray Train, who had been an ever-present in the Division One campaign, was out with a broken ankle for several weeks early in the season. Bobby Parker, also ever present in 1974-75, similarly missed a number of games with a tendon injury that he had first sustained while playing at Manchester City the previous March. Les O'Neill also suffered at times from injuries. Eddie Prudham also earned himself a run in the side until he too was injured, but one way and another it was the view of Herbert Nicholson, the physiotherapist who was also a long-time servant of the club, that 1975-76 was as bad a season as the club had ever had for injuries.

The injury problem was, of course, compounded by the fact that Carlisle only possessed a modestly sized squad. When the club played at Everton in the League Cup in October, the eleven players selected were virtually the only fit members of the entire playing staff. Hopelessly outplayed for the entire game, the wonder was that United lost only 0-2 and even then the second goal came in virtually the last minute. There was certainly no hint that the glorious visit to Goodison less than twelve months earlier was going to be repeated. The limited number of players available also meant that some of the fringe players in Division One, such as Mike McCartney and Mike Barry were now given more chances to shine. Barry's form in particular was one of the few bright spots in the grim early weeks of the season.

On 14 February 1976, United won 2-1 at bottom club York, a result remarkable partly for the fact that it pushed Carlisle seven rungs up the table to eleventh. The following weekend saw Bolton Wanderers come to Brunton Park as divisional leaders and, like Ipswich and Everton twelve months earlier, they were leaders no longer at the end of the game as Carlisle defeated them 3-2. Late in the game Eddie Spearritt scored the winning goal in what proved to be the only time he featured on the Carlisle scoresheet. Three days after the visit from the Trotters, it was the turn of Sunderland to come to Brunton Park. They were now top of the table on goal-difference from Bolton and Bristol City and by the end of the game they too had dropped down a place. Instead it was Bristol City who took over top spot by defeating Oldham 1-0 in their own game the same evening.

Carlisle and Sunderland meanwhile fought out a 2-2 draw, with the Carlisle equaliser coming in the final minutes from Mike Barry with one of his raking long-range drives. The attendance at Brunton Park that evening was 20,001, easily the best of the season and one swollen by the thousands of supporters who had travelled over from the North East for the game. Bob Stokoe was still the manager at Roker Park and three years after Sunderland's historic FA Cup victory he was keener than ever to steer the club back into the top flight. He was a long-time admirer of Ray Train, whose form in the 1974-75 season had earned him the Player of the Year accolade both from the fans in Carlisle and also from the London Branch of the supporters club. This offshoot had been formed in November 1974 after the QPR game and over 30 years later is still going strong.

Ray was, in common with a number of his teammates, keen to return to the top flight if possible, and if not with Carlisle United then with another club. In the week of the transfer deadline it was Sunderland who paid £90,000 for his services. Before long, Ray Train was a member of a Second Division championship team as the Black Cats finished three points clear of Bristol City and West Brom. As for Ray himself, he later moved to Bolton, winning another Second Division championship medal, and then cemented his reputation as a promotion mascot by helping Watford move up from Division Three. In all, he played for nine different clubs and made well over 500 League appearances in his career. For a number of years he was reserve-team coach, then chief scout at Middlesbrough, and still lives in the town, though he now scouts for West Brom.

Gradually the team line up at Brunton Park was changing. In February 1976 John Lathan had arrived from Mansfield to strengthen the midfield. He had been in the Stags' team that had lost to Carlisle in the FA Cup the previous year. In March the departure of Ray Train coincided with the arrival of Phil Bonnyman from Hamilton Academical. A cultured player who was not always appreciated as he should have been, he was later sold for a much larger fee than the £25,000 that Carlisle had expended. He and Lathan became first-team regulars as the club continued to suffer injury problems. Bobby Parker, Mike McCartney and Eddie Prudham were all long-term casualties who missed the last three months of the season. Results were patchy and it was only the defeat of Plymouth on the last day of the season that finally ensured Carlisle's Second Division survival. Dick Young expressed his relief: 'I've done the job I set out to do. We've avoided relegation and I'm quite happy about that. I'll be able to sleep tonight.'

When the club's retained list was published a few days after the end of the season, it was clear that more changes to the First Division squad were to be expected. Eddie Spearritt was given a free transfer, while Joe Laidlaw and Bobby Owen were put on the open-to-transfer list. Eddie Spearritt signed for Gillingham in the close season, thereby ending his two-year stint in the north. He later moved to Australia, first to play football before settling 'down under'.

When I spoke to Spearritt some years ago, he sounded as though he would easily fit into the cast of *Neighbours*, such was his accent. Joe Laidlaw, having been the club's top scorer in 1974-75, had found the going harder in the Second Division and his six League goals included three from the penalty spot. He was sold to Doncaster Rovers in the summer for £12,000, where he spent three seasons before further moves to Portsmouth, Hereford United and finally Mansfield Town. He settled in the Portsmouth area and his son Jamie is a useful player at non-league level.

Bobby Owen had reinvented himself as a centre-half in the latter part of the 1975-76 season and had played very well in that position. He would remain another year at Brunton Park but would scarcely feature in the first team in that last campaign. He went on loan at different times to Northampton, Workington and even his old club Bury for part of the season and in the summer of 1977 joined Doncaster on a free transfer, where he linked up with Joe Laidlaw. At Belle Vue his career took on a new lease of life and he was voted Player of the Year. He eventually moved back to the Bury area and I believe still visits Gigg Lane from time to time.

May 1976 saw a further change in life at Brunton Park when the Chairman EG Sheffield died after a short illness at the age of 62. George Sheffield had joined the board early in 1958 and became chairman less than two years later in November 1959. Despite his relatively patrician background, he had always been a Carlisle follower who, until his eleva- tion to the board, had preferred to watch from the terraces. He had played football for his Cambridge college and was also a keen sailor and golfer who was a former captain of Penrith Golf Club. One of his tenets was 'Don't buy what you cannot afford' and this view was an abiding principle of his time at Brunton Park. The club was in a poor financial position when he came onto the board and he made it a priority that the club should be put on a sound financial footing and pay its way. He was a very effective chairman who, though a quiet man, commanded great respect and his approach had a lot to do with the success of Carlisle United in his sixteen years at the helm.

David Dent was the club secretary for most of that time and it is worth recalling the comments he made about EG Sheffield at the time. 'Firstly there was his absolute and total sincerity and honesty in all his dealings. One was always left with a total belief in his word – his word could be taken as a gentleman. Then he had this very great ability to make people work for him out of affection. One always wanted to work for him. He also had this enormous calming influence that he could give to any situation. He always had an ability to prevent situations getting out of hand'. As for David Dent, he moved to Coventry City as secretary in 1978 and eventually became Secretary of the Football League. He still follows the progress of Carlisle United with interest while maintaining professional neutrality.

With the death of George Sheffield, it is perhaps worth considering whether or not Carlisle deserved to be relegated form Division One or indeed whether or not they could have stayed longer than they actually did. There is of course a certain tradition of unlikely teams from Glossop via Leyton Orient, Northampton Town, Carlisle United, Swindon Town etc who have managed a single 'Season in the Sun'. It is hard therefore not to feel that Carlisle were in some ways lucky to be promoted and could not really have expected to do much better than they did.

If the League table tells the true story, then Carlisle, with just 29 points – four fewer than anyone else – were certainly the worst team in the First Division. Carlisle only scored 43 times, which at the time was the lowest total by any United side in history. They won only twelve of their 42 matches. Yet to look behind the statistics, a different picture can emerge. If Carlisle United were the worst team, then champions Derby were the best and Carlisle took three points off them with a win and a draw. Chelsea scored only 42 goals and won just nine matches. Luton won just eleven and both Coventry and Leicester twelve apiece, the same as Carlisle. Moreover, Carlisle conceded just 59 goals. No fewer than eight teams had worse defensive records than United, including Burnley, who ended the season in eighth place.

Unfortunately, Carlisle lost 25 out of the 42 games played, which was four more than any other side in the First Division. The eleven home defeats and fourteen away from Brunton Park were both the worst totals in the League. The problem was compounded by the fact that sixteen of those defeats were by a single-goal margin. Six of them came from goals scored in the last five minutes. This included three matches in a row just after Christmas and both games against Newcastle. As Johnny Giles commented after Leeds' own narrow victory at Brunton Park, they had the experience to be able to win or at least draw games without playing at their best. Carlisle, in contrast, as Les Cocker observed, went for the win every time and they all too often came unstuck. With more experience, those losses of concentration might have been avoided, especially as Carlisle never won a game in the last five minutes. In 1973-74 they won two and lost one in that five-minute period which over a season seems a more reasonable average.

Goalscoring was an undoubted problem. It is generally acknowledged that the higher the division in which a team plays, the more likely they are to take any scoring opportunities offered to them. It is sometimes said that Carlisle United should have gone out and bought a proven '20 goals a season' striker who would have made the difference between staying up and going down. The problem with this theory is its impracticality. Carlisle players were all on the same basic wage with extras for appearing in the first team. The top scorers in the First Division that season were people like Malcolm MacDonald, Brian Kidd, Bob Latchford, Frank Worthington, Allan Clarke etc, who all cost very substantial transfer fees. Players like that would only have come to Brunton Park for a wage far in excess of that paid to the rest of the team. It is also worth noting that Malcolm MacDonald top-scored in the First Division with only 21 goals from 42 games, i.e. a goal every other game on average. Every team in the First Division would have wanted a '20 goals a season' striker but only Newcastle managed to possess one and they only finished fifteenth in the table.

Carlisle United achieved what they did based on sound financial management that is a tribute to the vision and acumen of George Sheffield and his fellow directors. Carlisle did break their transfer record in 1974 to buy Bobby Parker and it was money well spent. Previously they had bought Kenny Wilson in a record deal and that unfortunately was money less wisely spent. Eddie Prudham was bought during the season to reinforce the forward line but sadly he proved to be injury prone and the club never really got a lot out of him. Bigger clubs can afford to take these hits but Carlisle's financial base is always going to be limited. Even on the day of the opening home match, Carlisle's crowd was the lowest in the division, as was their average gate that season. In terms of catchment area, Carlisle's gates were probably among the highest but Carlisle United play their games in Carlisle, not a big metropolis, and many would say amen to that.

The alternative strategy would have been to go out and buy a 'hard man' as a 'midfield general' to stiffen the centre of the pitch. Again, such players do not grow on trees, although they are commoner than '20 goals a season' strikers. Yet again it was always difficult to attract 'top quality' players, or rather players with 'top quality reputations' to Carlisle for reasons outlined above.

Moreover, Carlisle had always been regarded as a team with a deserved reputation for playing good football, as epitomised in the 'push and run' style advocated and practised by Dick Young as the coach. It had taken them from the depths of the Fourth Division right up to the First. To have signed a 'hard man' purely for that purpose would have been a negation of that philosophy and for all that the club stood for. This is not to suggest that Carlisle did not have one or two players in their ranks that did not always take prisoners but in general Carlisle's position near the top of the 'Fair Play' League in 1974-75 tells its own story and should not be faulted.

With a little more 'savvy' in defending a lead, or at least the one point that they started out with, then yes, Carlisle could probably have survived the season but not with very much to spare. In the longer run it is hard to see how they could, given the financial resources available, have spent any length of time in the top flight.

Carlisle United in truth were probably punching above their weight in playing regular Second Division football let alone moving up to Division One. It is easier to lose a reputation than to acquire one but Carlisle's reputation for playing good football survived the 1974-75 season intact. In fact it was, if anything, enhanced by the exposure their play received in front of the country's leading players and managers, not to mention journalists. If Danny Blanchflower was right in saying that football is not so much about winning as about glory, then Carlisle United in 1974-75 did him proud.

We need, though, to conclude the story of Carlisle United and their time of glory. Soon after the death of George Sheffield, another figure departed from the stage as Bill Green moved south to join West Ham. Although his form had not been as commanding as twelve months earlier, Bill Green had remained the focus of attention from bigger clubs. The fee of £90,000 was much less than Tottenham had been willing to pay a year earlier. It was, however, still good business for a player who had cost a mere £15,000, though £50,000 of that sum was expended on bringing in Ian McDonald from St Johnstone as a replacement central defender. Bill Green subsequently moved to Peterborough, Chesterfield (where he and Phil Bonnyman once played in a team that won 6-2 at Brunton Park) and Doncaster Rovers. He has stayed in the football business and is now Director of Football at Wigan Athletic.

The 1976-77 season began for Carlisle with a surprise victory at the home of FA Cup-holders Southampton who had defeated Manchester United in an upset almost as great as the defeat of Leeds by Sunderland three years earlier. Carlisle's two goals at the Dell were scored by Billy Rafferty. He had been signed in the close season from Plymouth some four years after Alan Ashman had tried to buy him from Coventry. The result proved to be something of a false dawn and, by November, Carlisle United were back in the relegation zone. Dick Young, who by temperament was a coach and not a manager, resigned, though he stayed as assistant manager when Bobby Moncur took over as the new man at the helm. Like Dick Young, Moncur had been a defender but had different ideas on how the game should be played. In May 1977 Carlisle United again left the Second Division but this time it was to drop into Division Three for the first time since 1965.

By now, the survivors of the First Division campaign were becoming thinner on the ground. In November 1976 John Gorman had been sold to Tottenham Hotspur for £60,000. He had been the only ever-present in 1975-76 and was voted the club's Player of the Year for the third time in five seasons. He was, however, desperate to move back into the higher class of football he had experienced two seasons earlier and after a tribunal fixed his fee at £80,000 was finally sold for £60,000 to the London club. A glittering career should have followed but his playing days were cut short by injuries. He later entered the field of management and is now the boss at Northampton, having formerly managed Swindon Town and Wycombe Wanderers.

Les O'Neill retired at the end of the 1976-77 campaign. Fittingly, he scored with a typical twenty-yard strike in his and Carlisle's last game in the Second Division, played at Cardiff, which earned a valuable point.

United then needed Orient to lose their last home match to stay up. Unfortunately, they drew against Hull City by the same 1-1 scoreline that had promoted Carlisle three years earlier. Now the same result from Orient pushed the Cumbrians down into Division Three. Les O'Neill too has remained in the football and currently scouts for John Gorman at Northampton, having previously been chief scout at Swindon and at Blackpool where he now lives.

More of the team were soon heading from the exit door at Brunton Park. Eddie Prudham had enjoyed a loan spell at Workington in what proved to be their last Football League season. In the summer of 1977 he joined Stockport County, where he had three more successful years. He later joined the prison service and for many years has worked on the Isle of Wight.

Mike Barry was transferred to Bristol Rovers in September 1977 in exchange for Jimmy Hamilton. Mike had first played in the USA in the summer of 1975 and as part of the American Soccer boom he later moved to the USA on a permanent basis. He now lives in Columbus Ohio, where he runs a business and does some football coaching. Peter Carr also made his way across the Atlantic through his football prowess and has settled on Cape Cod in Massachusetts where he owns a motel. He still has family in the North East whom he comes to visit on a regular basis. The gifted Dennis Martin left Brunton Park a few weeks after Mike Barry, having been the subject of a surprise bid from Newcastle United. He, too, therefore managed to return to the First Division but it was a short stay and six months later he was transferred to Mansfield Town where his playing career finished. Eschewing the idea of remaining in football, he joined Pearl Insurance for whom he now works in Kettering.

Frank Clarke had been one of the older members of the team when he arrived at Brunton Park and he played his last game for Carlisle United in March 1978. For a while he remained at the club in a coaching capacity before returning to the Midlands and in particular to Shrewsbury. His playing career had begun there and he later ran a sports centre in the town.

Allan Ross was just a few weeks younger than Frank Clarke. Having seen off the challenge of Martin Burleigh, Rossie became the first and only Carlisle player to make over 500 senior appearances for the club. He retired at the end of the 1977-78 season by which time Trevor Swinburne had been signed and was the first-choice keeper. Rossie did make one last appearance in October 1978 to help out in an injury crisis and it is nice to record that he kept a clean sheet as Carlisle defeated Swindon 2-0.

After his retirement, he worked on the commercial side of the club for a while but spent most of his post-football days working for the housing department of Carlisle City Council. His untimely death at the age of 57 was widely mourned.

So, too, was the death in a car crash of Hugh Neil in November 1978. As chief scout and assistant manager to Dick Young, he had been an integral part of the Carlisle United set up since joining the club as a player in 1961. He was on a scouting mission when he was fatally injured in an accident near Glasgow when aged just 42. Among the other backroom staff, Herbert Nicholson died in 1984. Dick Young retired in 1977 but came back to the club when Bob Stokoe was reappointed manager in September 1980. He retired again some years later and died in his sleep in January 1989 at the age of 70.

Tot Winstanley had left Carlisle for Brighton and Hove Albion back in October 1974, having played just twice for United that season. In October 1979 he returned to Brunton Park to be reunited with Bobby Moncur, whom he had known from his Newcastle days. Tot retired at the end of that season but has settled in Carlisle where for a while he had his own building supplies business.

By now there were few survivors of the team that had graced Division One but Bobby Parker was still a constant presence in the United defence. Despite his Midland provenance, he has happily settled in the area and spent ten seasons at Brunton Park before he was given a free transfer. He played at Queen of the South for a while and for many years worked for Cavrays food processing factory in Carlisle where he became a health and safety officer. He now works in a similar capacity for Marks & Spencer.

Mike McCartney has also settled in Carlisle where he works in the building trade. He stayed at Brunton Park until the 1980 close season when Southampton bought him for £80,000. He too therefore returned to experience a season in the First Division until the following summer when he moved again to Plymouth Argyle. In March 1983, he returned to Brunton Park in a transfer that saw Gordon Staniforth, who in 1979 had become Carlisle's record buy, move in the opposite direction down to Home Park.

McCartney made the last of his 287 League appearances for Carlisle United in the 3-5 home defeat by Rotherham United on 27 December 1986, thereby ending the final playing link with the First Division team. It was his 358th League game in total but his playing career still had plenty of life in it. He moved to Gretna, then in the Northern League, where he spent twelve years as player-manager, making some 500 appearances for the club before suffering the fate of all football managers in January 2000. By then, his active playing days had exceeded all the other members of Carlisle's First Division side by well over a decade.

Epilogue

Saturday, 21 August 2004 dawned bright and sunny. For some five hundred football supporters, their journey from Carlisle and elsewhere down to the county of Gloucestershire, and in particular to the small town of Nailsworth near Stroud, would be a pleasant one. The attraction of Nailsworth on that particular day was that Carlisle United were due to play their third fixture in the Nationwide Conference that afternoon against Forest Green Rovers, the local football team.

It was 30 years earlier, to the very day, on Wednesday, 21 August 1974, that Carlisle and their fans had woken to learn that their team had, by dint of the previous evening's win at Middlesbrough, climbed to the top of the First Division. Admittedly, that particular period on top had been very brief. By that evening, Manchester City had returned to the top spot for the rest of the week until Carlisle reclaimed first place after defeating Tottenham Hotspur three days later.

Now, the team that once topped the English First Division was meeting on equal terms one which on that same date was scarcely making an impact in its own county league, let alone on a wider stage. Forest Green Rovers, whose origins date back further than those of Carlisle United, began life back in 1890 as 'Nailsworth and Forest Green Rovers'. For many years their horizons were limited to the immediate confines of their Gloucestershire surroundings. From first joining the Stroud and District League in 1902, they progressed to the Gloucestershire Northern Senior League in 1922, the Gloucestershire County League in 1968, the Hellenic League in 1975, the Southern League in 1982 and finally the Conference in 1998, where they remain. At the end of the 1973-74 campaign they had finished a modest tenth out of the eighteen teams in the Gloucestershire County League. The following season they would progress to sixth, but a full fifteen points behind the champions Matson Athletic. Nevertheless, their rise from the Gloucestershire County League to Conference has been almost as remarkable in its way as that of Carlisle United rising from the Fourth to the First Division.

Carlisle's Conference season had not begun particularly well. The first two games, at home to Canvey Island and away to Northwich Victoria, had produced two draws and only two goals scored. When they kicked off at the Lawn against Forest Green, they were lying below halfway in fourteenth place. The teams above included non-league stalwarts such as

Crawley Town and Tamworth, while Dagenham & Redbridge occupied top spot. Forest Green, however, had lost both their opening fixtures and were bottom of the table with no points and a goal-difference of minus five.

Carlisle United fans made up about half of the crowd of 1,071, which was well above the usual attendance at the Lawn. They were rewarded for their support with a 3-0 victory, Carlisle's first ever in the Conference. The win pushed them back into the top half of the table, a position they would never relinquish in the rest of the campaign. As for Forest Green, they lost ten of their opening eleven games, but thanks to Northwich Victoria's relegation on financial grounds, managed to survive in the Conference and they are still there today. They even, it must be admitted, won the return fixture at Brunton Park the following April, the only goal coming, as so often happens on such occasions, from an ex-Carlisle player in Damon Searle.

From the top of Division One, Carlisle United had travelled down as far as the lower half of the Conference. Arguably, this moment marked the end of 30 years of general decline. From that time onwards, the club's fortunes finally began to rise again. At the end of 2004-05, Carlisle United returned to the Football League after its one season in the Conference. Now it is back in League One, which I still sometimes tend to think of as the 'old' Third Division. The football landscape has changed hugely since Carlisle were in the 'old' First Division, not least with the advent in 1992 of the Premier League and all that has followed from that change in football governance. Nevertheless, I like to think that one day this book might have a sequel.

Guide to Seasonal Summaries

Col 1: Match number (for league fixtures); Round (for cup-ties).
        e.g. 4R means 'Fourth round replay.'

Col 2: Date of the fixture and whether Home (H), Away (A), or Neutral (N).

Col 3: Opposition.

Col 4: Attendances. Home gates appear in roman; Away gates in *italics*.
        Figures in **bold** indicate the largest and smallest gates, at home and away.
        Average home and away attendances appear after the final league match.

Col 5: Respective league positions of Carlisle and opponents after the game.
        Carlisle's position appears on the top line in roman.
        Their opponents' position appears on the second line in *italics*.
        For cup-ties, the division and position of opponents is provided.
        e.g. 2:12 means the opposition are twelfth in Division 2.

Col 6: The top line shows the result: W(in), D(raw), or L(ose).
        The second line shows Carlisle's cumulative points total.

Col 7: The match score, Carlisle's given first.
        Scores in **bold** show Carlisle's biggest league win and heaviest defeat.

Col 8: The half-time score, Carlisle's given first.

Col 9: The top line shows Carlisle's scorers and times of goals in roman.
        The second line shows opponents' scorers and times of goals in *italics*.
        A 'p' after the time of a goal denotes a penalty; 'og' an own-goal.
        The third line gives the name of the match referee.

Team line-ups: Carlisle's line-ups appear on top line, irrespective of whether
        they are home or away. Opposition teams are on the second line in *italics*.
        Players of either side who are sent off are marked !
        Carlisle's players making their league debuts are displayed in **bold**.

LEAGUE DIVISION 2 — Manager: Alan Ashman — SEASON 1973-74

Match details

No	H/A	Opponent	Date	Att	Pos	Pt	Res	F-A	H-T	Scorers, Times, and Referees
1	H	CARDIFF	25/8	6,863	10 *9*	1	D	1-1	1-0	Clarke F 9 / *Bell 85p* — Ref: A Jones
2	A	LUTON T	1/9	7,231	20 *9*	1	L	1-6	0-6	Owen 62 / *[Aston 23, Butlin 34] Finney 14, 20, Anderson 15, 25,* — Ref: D Nippard
3	H	NOTTS CO	8/9	6,109	15 *17*	3	W	3-0	0-0	Martin 80, O'Neill 86, 88 — Ref: A Morrissey
4	A	MIDDLESBROUGH	11/9	16,837	17 *3*	3	L	0-1	0-0	*Craggs 70* — Ref: H Davey
5	A	SHEFFIELD W	15/9	15,080	20 *11*	3	L	0-1	0-0	*Thompson 78* — Ref: G Hill
6	H	PORTSMOUTH	18/9	6,416	21 *13*	3	L	0-2	0-0	*Hiron 53, Davies 72* — Ref: P Willis
7	H	OXFORD U	22/9	5,093	19 *20*	5	W	2-1	0-0	Clarke F 53, Martin 70 / *Curran 48* — Ref: H Williams
8	A	MILLWALL	29/9	8,907	16 *14*	7	W	2-1	0-0	Kitchener 83 (og), Green 89 / *Bolland 80* — Ref: T Bosi
9	A	PORTSMOUTH	2/10	10,796	18 *17*	7	L	1-2	0-1	Owen 74 / *Hand 12, 88* — Ref: M Sinclair
10	H	BOLTON W	6/10	8,365	15 *12*	9	W	1-0	1-0	Owen 34 — Ref: E Wallace

Line-ups (Carlisle player / *opponent*)

No	1	2	3	4	5	6	7	8	9	10	11	12 sub used
1	Ross / *Irwin*	Carr / *Dwyer*	Gorman / *Bell*	Green / *Phillips*	Winstanley / *Murray*	O'Neill / *Smith*	Train / *Villars*	Ternent / *Reece*	Clarke F* / *Woodruff*	Laidlaw / *Showers*	Martin / *Anderson*	Delgado
2	Ross / *Horn*	Carr / *Shanks*	Gorman / *Thompson*	Green / *Anderson*	Winstanley / *Faulkner*	Train* / *Garner*	Martin / *Ryan Jimmy Ryan John*	Ternent / *Butlin*	Clarke F / *Finney*	Owen / *Finney*	Laidlaw / *Aston*	Delgado
3	Ross / *McManus*	Carr / *Brindley*	Gorman / *Worthington*	O'Neill / *Masson*	Green / *Needham*	Tiler / *Stubbs*	Martin / *Nixon*	Owen / *Bradd*	Clarke F / *Randall*	Delgado / *Probert*	Laidlaw* / *Carter*	Barry
4	Ross / *Platt*	Carr / *Craggs*	Gorman / *Spraggon*	Ternent / *Taylor**	Green / *Boam*	Tiler / *Maddren*	O'Neill / *Mills*	Barry / *McMordie*	Clarke F / *Hickton*	Laidlaw / *Foggon*	Martin / *Armstrong*	Delgado / *Souness*
5	Ross / *Springett*	Carr / *Rodrigues*	Gorman / *Shaw*	Tiler / *Thompson*	Green / *Craig J*	Ternent / *Craig T*	Martin / *Potts*	O'Neill* / *Prendergast*	Clarke F / *Joicey*	Laidlaw / *Sunley*	Barry / *Knighton*	Owen
6	Ross / *Mikins*	Carr / *Roberts*	Gorman / *Wilson*	Ternent / *Piper*	Green / *Stephenson*	Tiler / *Hand*	O'Neill / *Marinello*	Barry / *Kellard*	Laidlaw / *Davies**	Martin / *Lewis*	Balderstone / *Hiron*	Reynolds
7	Ross / *Burton*	Carr / *Lucas*	Gorman / *Shuker*	O'Neill / *Roberts*	Green / *Clark C*	Tiler / *Evanson*	Martin / *Clarke D*	Barry / *Fleming*	Clarke F / *Cassidy*	Laidlaw / *Curran*	Balderstone / *Aylott**	Atkinson
8	Ross / *King*	Carr / *Brown*	Gorman / *Cripps*	O'Neill / *Dorney*	Green / *Kitchener*	Tiler / *Saul*	Martin / *Bolland*	Barry / *Clark*	Clarke F / *Wood*	Laidlaw / *Dunphy*	Balderstone* / *Hill*	Delgado
9	Ross / *Mikins*	Carr / *Roberts*	Gorman / *Wilson*	O'Neill / *Piper*	Green / *Stephenson*	Tiler / *Hand*	Martin / *Marinello*	Barry / *Kellard*	Clarke F* / *Davies*	Delgado / *Lewis**	Laidlaw / *Hiron*	Owen / *Mellows*
10	Ross / *Siddall*	Carr / *Ritson*	Gorman / *McAllister*	O'Neill / *Rimmer*	Green / *Jones P*	Tiler / *Waldron*	Martin / *Byrom*	Barry! / *Darling*	Owen / *Greaves*	Balderstone / *Lee**	Laidlaw / *Phillips*	Nicholson

Match reports

1. United debutant Frank Clarke's 20 yard left-foot shot gives Carlisle an early lead. United continue to press and Clarke sets up opportunities for Green and O'Neill as well as himself but fail to take their chances. Bell's well-struck penalty after Reece is fouled gives Cardiff a late point.

2. Carlisle's defence is caught square and buried under an avalanche of six goals in a 20-minute spell. Anderson's left-foot drive being the pick. Ex-Hatters defender Delgado helps to steady the ship and Owen gets his third goal in two games. It is Carlisle's first ever defeat by Luton.

3. Barry's entry off the bench for his United debut transforms Carlisle's performance in a match that looks to be heading for stalemate. Martin's low shot breaks the deadlock. O'Neill scores with a fine strike from outside the area and then is on hand to head home a cross from Martin.

4. After an even first half, Middlesbrough gradually take control of the game. Armstrong hits the post before Cragg's fiercely hit free-kick flies past keeper Ross. Green fouls Mills in the area but Hickton's spot-kick hits the outside of the post before rebounding for an eventual goal-kick.

5. The Carlisle defence, well marshalled by Green and Ternent, frustrates the Owls for the bulk of the game. Carlisle however fail to make the most of their few opportunities and pay the penalty when following Craig's corner, Thompson forces the ball home after a goalmouth melee.

6. The return of Balderstone fails to inspire United who look sluggish up front. Balderstone's own influence fades in the second half as Hiron puts the visitors into the lead with a close-range header. Davies heads in the second from Hiron's pass for Pompey's first win of the campaign.

7. Carlisle, with a more influential Balderstone on form, have the better of the first half. Curran's direct free-kick gives a surprise lead to the visitors but Balderstone sets up Clarke for the equaliser. Martin's low shot seals a win for the home side after receiving Carr's neat pass.

8. Bolland's strike from outside the area comes just after O'Neill has hit the woodwork for Carlisle. A minute later Kitchener's own-goal gifts an equaliser to the visitors. Green heads the winning goal for Carlisle right at the death to give United their first win at the Den in thirteen visits.

9. Hand puts the home side ahead with a half-volley from the edge of the area. Martin hits the woodwork before substitute Owen levels things from O'Neill's cross. Hand grabs the winning goal with two minutes left with another half-volley after Davies neatly wins the ball in the air.

10. Barry's dismissal after 23 minutes for retaliation against Rimmer galvanises the home side and soon afterwards Laidlaw with a decisive centre sets up Owen for the only goal. Bolton dominate most of the second half and Ritson's shot hits the woodwork late on but Carlisle just survive.

No	Venue	Opponent	Date	HT	FT	Res	Pos			Att
11	A	WEST BROMWICH	13/10	1-0	1-1	D	12	17	10	12,528
12	A	CRYSTAL PALACE	20/10	0-0	1-0	W	12	22	12	19,678
13	H	MIDDLESBROUGH	23/10	0-1	1-1	D	10	1	13	11,152
14	H	FULHAM	27/10	2-0	3-0	W	7	15	15	7,147
15	A	SWINDON T	3/11	2-1	2-2	D	9	21	16	6,480
16	H	HULL C	10/11	1-0	4-0	W	6	12	18	6,563
17	A	NOTTINGHAM F	17/11	0-2	0-2	L	9	4	18	11,153
18	H	BRISTOL C	24/11	1-1	2-1	W	8	9	20	6,020
19	H	BLACKPOOL	8/12	1-1	2-3	L	12	7	20	6,641
20	A	ORIENT	15/12	0-0	1-0	W	10	3	22	7,645
21	H	MILLWALL	22/12	1-1	1-0	D	10	16	23	8,300

---

11 — A WEST BROMWICH — 13/10 — D 1-1
Owen 36 / Brown T 50
Ref: D Smith
Carlisle: Ross, Carr, Gorman, O'Neill, Green, Tiler, Martin, Barry, Owen, Clarke T, Laidlaw
Opponents: Latchford, Nisbet, Merrick, Cantello, Wile, Robertson, Johnston, Brown A, Brown T, Hartford, Shaw

Laidlaw's pin point cross from a Gorman pass allows Owen to head Carlisle into a first-half lead. Keeper Clarke in his first game of the season is penalised for steps and Brown lashes home a right-foot drive after the resulting free kick. Green's goal-line clearance keeps the score level.

12 — A CRYSTAL PALACE — 20/10 — W 1-0
Laidlaw 80
Ref: J Taylor
Carlisle: Ross, Carr, Gorman, O'Neill, Green, Tiler, Martin, Barry, Owen, Clarke F, Laidlaw
Opponents: Hammond, Wall, Taylor T, Jeffries, Barry, Blyth, Cannon, Cooke, Possee, Rogers, Taylor P

Without a home win since March, bottom of the table Palace begin brightly but by half-time United have come closest to scoring when a great save by Hammond denies Laidlaw. Laidlaw's fine solo goal is decisive, though Rogers' clever free-kick later draws a full-length save by Ross.

13 — H MIDDLESBROUGH — 23/10 — D 1-1
Martin 80 / Foggon 3
Ref: E Garner
Carlisle: Ross, Carr, Gorman, O'Neill, Green, Tiler, Martin, Barry, Owen, Clarke F, Laidlaw
Opponents: Platt, Craggs, Spraggon, Souness !, Boam, Maddren, Murdoch, Mills, Hickton, Foggon, Armstrong

Foggon's neat goal from a Souness pass puts the table-topping visitors in control. An off the ball incident leads to Souness's dismissal and ex-Boro star Laidlaw hits the visitors' crossbar. Martin's equaliser takes a slight deflection just when it seems the visitors will steal both points.

14 — H FULHAM — 27/10 — W 3-0
Clarke F 25, Martin 29, O'Neill 47
Ref: J Williams
Carlisle: Ross, Carr, Gorman, O'Neill, Green, Tiler, Martin, Terment, Owen, Clarke F, Laidlaw
Opponents: Mellor, Cutbush, Slough, Mullery, Went, Lacey, Dunne, Busby, Mitchell*, Lloyd, Barrett, Earle

An early 'goal' by Busby is narrowly ruled out for offside before Gorman's long run and cross gives Clarke an easy header for the opener. A shot from Martin that the keeper should have saved then slips past Mellor in the Fulham goal. O'Neill heads the third from Martin's neat chip.

15 — A SWINDON T — 3/11 — D 2-2
Clarke F 5, 10 / Eastoe 8, 46
Ref: R Tinkler
Carlisle: Ross, Carr, Gorman, O'Neill, Green, Tiler, Martin, Barry, Owen, Clarke F, Laidlaw
Opponents: Allan, Thomas, Stroud, Butler, Burrows, Gabriel, Moss, McGovern, Eastoe*, Syrett, Jenkins, Clarke

Clarke puts Carlisle ahead, pouncing after Laidlaw's shot is half-saved. On-loan Eastoe equalises from close range before Clarke nets again, this time taking advantage of Thomas' poor pass. Eastoe is gifted a second equaliser after Ross misjudges a cross before defences take control.

16 — H HULL C — 10/11 — W 4-0
Owen 29, Martin 49, Laidlaw 75, 90
Ref: R Capey
Carlisle: Ross, Carr, Gorman, Terment, Winstanley, Tiler, Martin, Balderstone, Owen, Clarke F, Laidlaw
Opponents: Wealands, Banks, Devries, Burnett, Deere, Galvin, Hawley*, Lord, Pearson, Wagstaff, Greenwood, McGill

Owen opens the scoring with a typically powerful volley from a Laidlaw knock-down. Martin slots home from close in after Laidlaw's header hits the bar. Laidlaw then exploits slack defending himself to double the score and to extend Carlisle's exciting unbeaten run to seven games.

17 — A NOTTINGHAM F — 17/11 — L 0-2
Martin 6, McKenzie 34
Ref: T Spencer
Carlisle: Ross, Carr, Gorman, O'Neill, Winstanley, Terment, Martin, Clarke F, Owen, Balderstone, Laidlaw
Opponents: Baron, O'Kane, Serela, Chapman, Cottam, Lyall, McKenzie, Richardson, Martin, McIntosh, Bowyer

Martin gives Forest an early lead following a move inspired by McKenzie. Forest are on fire and McKenzie, the Division's leading scorer adds to his total from a McIntosh cross. The second half is more even but despite the efforts of O'Neill in particular, Carlisle cannot break through.

18 — H BRISTOL C — 24/11 — W 2-1
Winstanley 14, O'Neill 75 / Ritchie 36
Ref: H Hackney
Carlisle: Ross, Carr, Gorman, O'Neill, Winstanley, Terment, Martin, Balderstone, Owen, Clarke F*, Laidlaw
Opponents: Bond, Tainton, Merrick, Sweeney, Rogers, Collier, Whitehead*, Ritchie, Gillies, Gow, Emanuel, Drysdale

Winstanley puts Carlisle ahead after Balderstone's free-kick hits the upright. City reply when Ritchie's volley from a Whitehead feed gives Ross no chance. O'Neill scores with a low drive after his first effort is blocked. The crossbar denies Laidlaw's header from Owen's cross.

19 — H BLACKPOOL — 8/12 — L 2-3
Train 43, O'Neill 76 / Bentley 41, Suddick 69, Alcock 87
Ref: M Lowe
Carlisle: Ross, Carr, Gorman, O'Neill, Green, Tiler, Martin, Balderstone, Owen, Train, Laidlaw
Opponents: Burridge, Curtis, Hatton, Alcock, James, Suddaby, Burns, Suddick, Dyson, Bentley, Walsh

Bentley's 35-yard strike gives the Seasiders the lead. Train's equaliser is then countered by Suddick before O'Neill levels the score with a full-length header header after first hitting the woodwork. Alcock's late winner from a Dyson pass gives the visitors a fourth win in six visits to Carlisle.

20 — A ORIENT — 15/12 — W 1-0
Martin 81
Ref: A Grey
Carlisle: Ross, Winstanley, Gorman, O'Neill, Green, Tiler*, Martin, Train, Owen, Balderstone, Laidlaw
Opponents: Goddard, Hoadley, Roffey, Allen, Harris, Walley, Fairbrother, Brisley, Bullock, Downing, Heppolette, McCartney

United fight a rearguard action for much of the match as Orient look to sustain their promotion challenge. Carlisle come into the game more in the second half and Martin's snap shot earns a valuable win. McCartney makes his league debut while Fairbrother has a late effort disallowed.

21 — H MILLWALL — 22/12 — D 1-1
Owen 4 / Wood 70
Ref: L Hayes
Carlisle: Ross, Winstanley, Gorman, Tiler, Green, Train, Martin, Owen, Owen, Clarke F, Laidlaw
Opponents: King, Donaldson, Jones, Dorney, Kitchener, Alder*, Saul, Clark, Wood, Balland, Hill, Kelly

Owen's smart header from a Clarke cross gives United an early lead but the home side fail to add to their tally. They pay for their profligacy when Wood nods in Hill's cross from close range. The size of the crowd disappoints as Sunderland FA Cup-tie vouchers are being given out.

LEAGUE DIVISION 2 — Manager: Alan Ashman — SEASON 1973-74

No	V	Opponent	Date	Att	Pos	Pt	Res	F-A	H-T	Scorers, Times, and Referees	1	2	3	4	5	6	7	8	9	10	11	12 sub used
22	A	PRESTON N E	26/12	11,446	16	25	7 W	1-0	0-0	Train 72. Ref: A Morrissey. Carlisle dominate the first period without creating many clear chances though the Carlisle defence has little problem containing the North End attack. After the interval Bruce hits the post before Train's speculative 30-yard shot deceives the Preston keeper; Clarke nearly adds a second.	Ross	Winstanley	Gorman	O'Neill	Green	Tiler	Martin	Train	Owen	Clarke F	Laidlaw	
											Healey	*McMahon*	*Snooks*	*Bird*	*Hawkins*	*Stiles*	*Sadler*	*Bruce*	*Holden*	*Burns*	*Williams*	
23	A	NOTTS CO	29/12	10,209	8	27	7 W	3-0	2-0	Laidlaw 4, 6 McVay 67 (og). Ref: M Kerkhof. Laidlaw's two early strikes at once put Carlisle in control, the first from a Train pass and the second being a lob over the keeper. County come into the game more after the break but McVay's own-goal seals their fate after he can only help another Laidlaw effort into his own net.	Ross	Winstanley	Gorman	Train	Green	Tiler	Martin	O'Neill	Owen	Clarke F	Laidlaw	
											Brown	*Brindley*	*Worthington*	*Masson*	*Needham*	*McVay*	*Nixon*	*Randall*	*Bradd**	*Probert*	*Collier*	
24	H	LUTON T	1/1	9,255	3	29	4 W	2-0	0-0	Green 55, Martin 70. Ref: J Goggins. After an even first half with few chances to either side, Green heads home at the near post from a Martin centre. Martin adds the second goal himself after his own header strikes the woodwork, after Laidlaw had made the opening. The win keeps Carlisle up in the promotion hunt.	Ross	Winstanley	Gorman	O'Neill*	Green	Tiler	Martin	Train	Owen	Clarke F	Laidlaw	Balderstone
											Horn	*Shanks*	*Thomson*	*Anderson*	*Faulkner*	*Garner*	*Ryan Jimmy*	*West*	*Butlin*	*Husband*	*Aston**	*Ryan John*
25	H	SHEFFIELD W	12/1	7,332	20	30	4 D	2-2	1-2	Laidlaw 35, Owen 90; Coyle 14, Mullen 34. Ref: J Whalley. Coyle makes use of slack defending to put the visitors ahead. Mullen is unmarked as he heads in the second from a Cameron cross. Laidlaw pulls one back with a powerful strike and Owen's late goal from Balderstone's through ball rewards heavy United pressure after the interval.	Ross	Carr	Gorman	O'Neill	Green	Balderstone	Martin*	Train	Owen	Clarke F	Laidlaw	McCartney
											Springett	*Cameron*	*Knighton*	*Thompson*	*Eustace*	*Mullen*	*Henderson*	*Coyle*	*Joicey*	*Craig T*	*Sunley*	
26	A	CARDIFF C	19/1	10,797	14	31	4 D	2-2	0-1	Train 47, Clarke F 87; McCulloch 45, Phillips 58. Ref: H New. Train's superb right-foot shot cancels out McCulloch's strike, following a half-saved shot from Phillips. Phillips' opportunism is rewarded by a second close-range goal before Clarke knocks in Owen's cross. It is only Carlisle's third point in nine visits to Cardiff's Ninian Park ground.	Ross	Carr	Gorman	O'Neill	Green	Balderstone	Martin	Train	Owen	Clarke F	Laidlaw	
											Irwin	*Dwyer*	*Bell*	*Impey*	*Murray*	*Villars*	*Farrington*	*McCulloch*	*Phillips**	*Carlin*	*Anderson*	*Reece*
27	H	ORIENT	2/2	9,422	2	33	4 W	3-0	2-0	Clarke 5, 41, Laidlaw 80. Ref: R Lee. Clarke heads in Balderstone's free-kick after Orient are guilty of slack marking. His second is nodded in from a Laidlaw cross and Clarke also hits the bar soon afterwards. Orient never give up but Laidlaw bangs in the third when left clear in front of goal before the BBC MoD cameras.	Ross	Carr	Gorman	O'Neill	Green	Balderstone	Martin	Train	Owen	Clarke F	Laidlaw	Hoppolette
											Jackson	*Payne*	*Boyle*	*Allen**	*Hoadley*	*Walley*	*Fairbrother*	*Brisley*	*Bullock*	*Queen*	*Downing*	*Downing*
28	A	BOLTON W	23/2	16,675	13	33	5 L	0-2	0-1	Byrom 29, Jones G 67p. Ref: J Yates. Leading scorer Byrom puts Bolton ahead with a scrappy goal after Carlisle fail to clear a cross. A hotly disputed penalty after Whatmore is challenged by Green enables Gary Jones to extend Bolton's lead. Ross is tested as Whatmore and Gary Jones both come close to another goal.	Ross	Carr	Gorman	Ternent	Green	Balderstone	Martin	Train	Owen	Clarke F	Laidlaw	
											Siddall	*Ritson*	*Dunne*	*McAllister*	*Jones P*	*Nicholson*	*Byrom*	*Greaves*	*Jones G*	*Whatmore*	*Thompson*	
29	H	WEST BROMWICH	25/2	6,407	5	33	6 L	0-1	0-1	Johnston 35. Ref: P Willis. On their first league visit to Brunton Park, West Brom look much the sharper side throughout the game. The only goal comes from an unlucky Balderstone error that Hartford seizes upon to set up Johnston for the decisive strike. The Baggies overtake Carlisle in the promotion race.	Ross	Carr	Gorman	Ternent	Green	Balderstone	Martin	Train	Owen	Clarke F*	Laidlaw	McCartney
											Latchford	*Nisbet*	*Thompson*	*Cantello*	*Wile*	*Robertson*	*Johnston*	*Brown T*	*Astle*	*Hartford**	*Glover*	*Donaghy*
30	H	PRESTON N E	2/3	7,671	18	34	7 D	2-2	0-2	O'Neill 62, Owen 78; Elwiss 14, 41. Ref: J Hough. Elwiss on his Preston debut puts the visitors ahead following hesitancy in the home defence and he doubles the lead after a Stiles through ball. O'Neill hits the post and Clarke the bar before O'Neill puts away Train's cross and Owen's equaliser owes much to Laidlaw's shrewd pass.	Ross	Brown	Gorman	O'Neill	Green	Tiler	Train	Balderstone	Owen	Clarke F	Laidlaw	
											Brown	*McMahon*	*McNab*	*Bird*	*Sadler*	*Baxter*	*Stiles*	*Lamb*	*Burns*	*Elwiss*	*Treacy*	
31	A	FULHAM	9/3	6,731	12	36	6 W	2-0	1-0	Laidlaw 32, Clarke F 85. Ref: W Gow. Barrett and Lacy miss early chances for Fulham before Laidlaw scores with an emphatic shot from Clarke's through ball. Carlisle dominate the second half and seal a fourth win in London this season when Clarke pursues a long ball and lobs the advancing Mellor in the Fulham goal.	Ross	Carr	Gorman	O'Neill	Green	Tiler	Martin	Train	Owen	Clarke F	Laidlaw	
											Mellor	*Fraser*	*Strong*	*Slough*	*Dunne*	*Lacy*	*Conway Jim*	*Friend**	*Bushby*	*Lloyd*	*Barrett*	*Conway John*

Football season results table (matches 32–42).

32. ASTON VILLA (A) — 13/3 · Pos 6 · L 1–2 (HT 0–1) · Att 12,007 · [14] · Pts 36
Scorers: Clarke F 75 | Evans 23, Hamilton 55p
Ref: R Challis

Pos	1	2	3	4	5	6	7	8	9	10	11
Carlisle	Ross	Carr	Gorman	O'Neill	Green	Tiler	Martin	Train	Owen	Clarke F	Laidlaw
Villa	Cumbes	Gidman	McDonald	McMahon	Nicholl	Turnbull	Little	Ross	Morgan	Hamilton	Evans

Laidlaw nearly scores early on, seizing on McMahon's back-pass but the home side takes the lead through Evans' 25-yard half-volley. Tiler concedes a penalty against his old club with a foul on Little, and Hamilton nets easily. Turnbull's error lets in Clarke who reduces the deficit.

---

33. CRYSTAL PALACE (H) — 16/3 · Pos 4 · W 1–0 (HT 1–0) · Att 6,964 · [21] · Pts 38
Scorers: Clarke F 26
Ref: I Smith

Pos	1	2	3	4	5	6	7	8	9	10	11
Carlisle	Ross	Carr	Gorman	O'Neill	Green	Balderstone	Martin	Train	Owen	Clarke F	Laidlaw
Palace	Hammond	Mulligan	Jump	Blyth	Barry	Johnson	Passee	Jeffries	Hill	Rogers	Taylor P

Good work by Owen and Laidlaw enable Clarke to open the score with an easy finish. Carlisle continue to dominate but Hammond's inspired form and poor shooting keep the score to a single goal. Rogers and Taylor have chances to equalise but complacency is Carlisle's main enemy.

---

34. HULL CITY (A) — 23/3 · Pos 5 · D 1–1 (HT 1–0) · Att 6,137 · [10] · Pts 39
Scorers: Owen 35 | Grimes 68
Ref: K Burns

Pos	1	2	3	4	5	6	7	8	9	10	11
Carlisle	Ross	Carr	Gorman	O'Neill	Green	Balderstone	Martin	Train	Owen	Clarke F	Laidlaw
Hull	Wealands	Banks	Devries	Grimes	Deere	Burnett	McGill	Lord	Pearson	Wagstaff	Greenwood

Owen keeps United's promotion hopes alive with a volley from Green's knock-down. Hull with Pearson prominent come back strongly after the interval and Grimes taps in after Pearson hits the post. Both sides struggle in the blustery conditions and are content with a point apiece.

---

35. SWINDON T (H) — 30/3 · Pos 4 · W 5–1 (HT 2–0) · Att 6,544 · [22] · Pts 41
Scorers: Clarke 2, 11, 69p, 76, Laidlaw 55 | Syrett 88
Ref: A Jones

Pos	1	2	3	4	5	6	7	8	9	10	11
Carlisle	Ross	Carr	Gorman	O'Neill	Green	Balderstone	Martin	Train	Owen	Clarke F	Laidlaw
Swindon	Allan	Dixon	Trollope	McLaughlin	Potter	Stroud	Moss	Syrett	Eastoe	Butler	Clarke* (McGovern)

Without an away win all season, Swindon struggle as Clarke scores twice early on, the second from Martin's cross. Laidlaw's diving header is followed by two more Clarke efforts, Eastoe conceding the penalty. Syrett, who has earlier hit the post, scores after Balderstone fails to clear.

---

36. BRISTOL C (A) — 6/4 · Pos 5 · L 0–2 (HT 0–1) · Att 9,570 · [16] · Pts 41
Scorers: — | Cheesley 29, Gillies 75
Ref: J Taylor

Pos	1	2	3	4	5	6	7	8	9	10	11
Carlisle	Ross	Carr	Gorman	McCartney	Green	Balderstone	Martin	Train	Owen	Clarke F	Laidlaw
Bristol C	Cashley	Sweeney	Drysdale	Gow	Collier	Merrick	Tainton*	Hunt	Cheesley	Gillies	Emanuel (Fear)

Carlisle play their usual neat football but Cheesley scores his debut goal with a powerful header from Tainton's corner to put City into the lead. Owen has a point-blank volley saved before Gillies scores the second, cutting through the Carlisle defence to score from a very narrow angle.

---

37. SUNDERLAND (A) — 12/4 · Pos 6 · L 1–2 (HT 0–0) · Att 34,179 · [5] · Pts 41
Scorers: Laidlaw 46 | Halom 50, Hughes 70
Ref: J Rice

Pos	1	2	3	4	5	6	7	8	9	10	11
Carlisle	Ross	Carr	Winstanley	O'Neill	Green	Balderstone	Martin	Train	Owen	Clarke F	Laidlaw
Sunderland	Montgomery	Malone	Bolton	Longhorn	Watson	Belfitt	Kerr	Hughes	Halom	Porterfield	Towers

After a quiet first half, Laidlaw opens the scoring after dispossessing the otherwise dependable Watson and slotting the ball home. Halom's reply is a decisive strike from the edge of the area. Hughes adds the second by beating Ross to Towers' astute chip through the United defence.

---

38. NOTTINGHAM F (H) — 13/4 · Pos 4 · W 2–1 (HT 0–1) · Att 9,258 · [8] · Pts 43
Scorers: Owen 70, Laidlaw 75 | McKenzie 41
Ref: P Baldwin

Pos	1	2	3	4	5	6	7	8	9	10	11
Carlisle	Ross	Carr	Winstanley	O'Neill	Green	Balderstone	Martin	Train	Owen	Gorman	Laidlaw
Nottingham F	Peacock	O'Kane	Winfield	Chapman	Cottam	Serella	McKenzie	Lyall	O'Neill	Bowyer	Dennehy* (McIntosh)

Against the run of play, Forest take the lead through O'Neill who intercepts to put McKenzie through to beat Ross. Owen, having missed earlier, powers in a header from Carr's cross. Laidlaw then produces a great solo goal, slicing through the defence to shoot past Peacock.

---

39. SUNDERLAND (H) — 16/4 · Pos 5 · W 1–0 (HT 0–0) · Att 19,692 · [9] · Pts 45
Scorers: Balderstone 55p
Ref: R Capey

Pos	1	2	3	4	5	6	7	8	9	10	11
Carlisle	Ross	Carr	Winstanley	O'Neill	Green	Balderstone	Martin	Train	Owen	Clarke F	Laidlaw
Sunderland	Montgomery	Malone	Guthrie	Longhorn	Watson	Belfitt	Kerr	Hughes	Halom	Porterfield	Ashurst* (Bolton)

The game turns on the penalty award after Ashurst is judged to have brought down Laidlaw inside the box. Balderstone beats Montgomery decisively. Beforehand, Longhorn had hit the post for the visitors who continue to press but in vain. It is United's best league gate since 1951.

---

40. BLACKPOOL (A) — 20/4 · Pos 5 · L 0–4 (HT 0–2) · Att 15,777 · [3] · Pts 45
Scorers: — | Dyson 11, Alcock 42, 56, Suddick 60p
Ref: D Biddle

Pos	1	2	3	4	5	6	7	8	9	10	11
Carlisle	Ross	Carr	Gorman	O'Neill	Green	Balderstone	Martin	Train	Owen	Clarke F	Laidlaw
Blackpool	Burridge	Hatton	Harrison	Alcock	James	Suddaby	Burns	Bentley	Dyson	Evanson*	Ainscow

Laidlaw's early 30-yard drive raps the crossbar before the unmarked Dyson scores with a header. Owen too hits the woodwork before Alcock's 25-yarder gives Ross no chance. Alcock nets again with a powerfully placed header and Suddick's penalty comes after Gorman fouls Alcock.

---

41. OXFORD U (A) — 23/4 · Pos 4 · W 1–0 (HT 0–0) · Att 9,675 · [17] · Pts 47
Scorers: Owen 87
Ref: K Baker

Pos	1	2	3	4	5	6	7	8	9	10	11
Carlisle	Ross	Carr	Gorman	O'Neill	Winstanley	Balderstone	Martin	Train	Owen	Clarke F	Laidlaw
Oxford U	Burton	Light	Shuker	Roberts	Clarke C	Briggs	Skeen	Fleming	Curran	Bray	Aylott

Oxford look the sharper in the early exchanges as Bray and Roberts go close before Carlisle dominate the rest of the encounter. Laidlaw in particular is in superb form but the home side almost holds out. Balderstone's free-kick is touched on to Owen who volleys home with power.

---

42. ASTON VILLA (H) — 27/4 · Pos 3 · W 2–0 (HT 1–0) · Att 12,494 · [14] · Pts 49
Scorers: Laidlaw 11, Clarke F 66
Ref: J Williams

Pos	1	2	3	4	5	6	7	8	9	10	11
Carlisle	Ross	Carr	Gorman	O'Neill	Winstanley	Balderstone	Martin	Train	Owen	Clarke F	Laidlaw
Villa	Cumbes	Robson	McDonald	McMahon	Nicholl	Ross	Graydon	Campbell*	Morgan	Hamilton	Little (Vowden)

In a match that could decide United's promotion fate, Laidlaw puts Carlisle ahead when set up by Clarke. Villa combine to hit the woodwork through McMahon and Graydon. Clarke meets Martin's cross to head the second goal to put Carlisle into a promotion spot for the first time.

Home 8,271 · Away 12,359 · Average 12,359

LEAGUE DIVISION 2 (CUP-TIES)

Manager: Alan Ashman

SEASON 1973-74

League Cup

			Att	F-A	H-T	Scorers, Times, and Referees	1	2	3	4	5	6	7	8	9	10	11	12 sub used
1	H	WORKINGTON 10 D	7,040 4:16	2:2	0:2	Owen 52, 57; Helliwell 20, McDonald 25; Ref: P Baldwin	Ross	Carr	Gorman	Ternent	Green	Winstanley	Train	Owen	Clarke F	Laidlaw	Martin	
						Rogan	*Ogilvie*	*Heslop*	*Geidmintis*	*Walker*	*Wood*	*Hall*	*Tyrer*	*Murphy*	*McDonald*	*Helliwell**	*Banks*

Despite the loss through suspension of Martin, the Reds take the game to Carlisle and Helliwell exploits hesitation in the Carlisle defence to open the scoring. McDonald then hits the second from 30 yards. Owen's brace owes much to Clarke, whose aerial power sets up both goals.

			Att	F-A	H-T	Scorers, Times, and Referees	1	2	3	4	5	6	7	8	9	10	11	12 sub used
1R	A	WORKINGTON 20 W	4,931 4:17	1:0	1:0	O'Neill 6; Ref: P Baldwin	Ross	Carr	Gorman	Delgado	Green	Tiler	O'Neill	Owen	Clarke F	Laidlaw	Martin	
						Rogan	*Ogilvie*	*Heslop*	*Geidmintis*	*Walker*	*Wood*	*Tyrer*	*Murphy*	*Martin*	*McDonald*	*Kisby**	*Rowlands*

O'Neill's scrambled effort early on gives Carlisle a first away win for eight months. The home side hits the woodwork through both Kisby with a centre and Murphy following a diagonal cross and look to be denied a penalty when Martin is brought down near the end by Delgado.

			Att	F-A	H-T	Scorers, Times, and Referees	1	2	3	4	5	6	7	8	9	10	11	12 sub used
2	A	GILLINGHAM 15 W	7,871 4:13	2:1	1:1	Balderstone 9, Martin 58; Richardson 20; Ref: P Reeves	Ross	Carr	Gorman	O'Neill	Green	Tiler	Martin	Barry	Owen	Balderstone*	Laidlaw	Delgado
						Gibson	*Lindsey*	*Peach*	*Quirke*	*Hill*	*Jacques*	*Tydeman*	*Jacks*	*Richardson*	*Wilks*	*Yeo*	

A rare headed goal by Balderstone from Owen's cross gives Carlisle an early lead. Wilks sets up Richardson for the equaliser before Martin's interception of Quirke's pass gives Carlisle the winner. Peach hits a post, while a clash of heads with Quirke causes Balderstone to be subbed.

			Att	F-A	H-T	Scorers, Times, and Referees	1	2	3	4	5	6	7	8	9	10	11	12 sub used
3	H	MANCHESTER C 9 L	14,472 1:11	0:1	0:0	Lee 82; Ref: V James	Ross	Carr	Gorman	O'Neill	Green	Tiler*	Martin	Balderstone	Owen	Clarke F	Laidlaw	Barry
						MacRae	*Pardoe*	*Donachie*	*Doyle*	*Booth*	*Oakes*	*Carrodus*	*Bell*	*Summerbee*	*Lee*	*Towers*	

Carlisle begin brightly despite losing Tiler through injury, forcing a series of corners. City hit the bar through Towers but the woodwork later denies both Clarke and Laidlaw. Lee scores a breakaway goal in the closing minutes, after a through ball from Carrodus had evaded Green.

FA Cup

			Att	F-A	H-T	Scorers, Times, and Referees	1	2	3	4	5	6	7	8	9	10	11	12 sub used
3	H	SUNDERLAND 4 D	20,595 2:12	0:0	0:0	Ref: P Partridge	Ross	Winstanley	Gorman	O'Neill	Green	Tiler*	Martin	Train	Owen	Clarke F	Laidlaw	Balderstone
						Montgomery	*Malone*	*Bolton*	*Horswill*	*Watson*	*Young*	*Kerr*	*Belfitt**	*Halom*	*Porterfield*	*Tueart*	*Hegan*

Carlisle look more dangerous early on as Martin and Clarke both have chances. Tiler goes off injured while Halom's long-range strike against the bar nearly gives Sunderland the lead. The second half, too, is evenly matched, although Green and Clarke go mighty close for Carlisle.

			Att	F-A	H-T	Scorers, Times, and Referees	1	2	3	4	5	6	7	8	9	10	11	12 sub used
3R	A	SUNDERLAND 4 W	25,710 2:12	1:0	0:0	Martin 68; Ref: P Partridge	Ross	Carr	Gorman	O'Neill	Green	Tiler*	Martin	Train	Owen	Clarke F	Laidlaw	Hegan
						Montgomery	*Malone*	*Bolton*	*Ashurst*	*Watson*	*Young*	*Kerr*	*Belfitt**	*Halom*	*Porterfield*	*Tueart*	

Sunderland begin positively and Halom forces Ross to make a fine save. The Carlisle keeper is the busier, foiling Watson, Porterfield and Belfitt at times but Martin's instinctive shot, after Train makes an opening, eliminates the FA Cup holders in the first defence of their trophy.

			Att	F-A	H-T	Scorers, Times, and Referees	1	2	3	4	5	6	7	8	9	10	11	12 sub used
4	A	LIVERPOOL 4 D	47,211 1:2	0:0	0:0	Ref: J Taylor	Ross	Carr	Gorman	O'Neill	Green	Balderstone	Martin	Train	Owen	Clarke F	Laidlaw	Callaghan
						Clemence	*Smith*	*Lindsay*	*Thompson*	*Lloyd*	*Hughes*	*Keegan*	*Cormack*	*Toshack*	*Boersma*	*Callaghan*	

In a one-sided encounter, Carlisle frustrate a Liverpool team that fails to score at home for the first time all season. Green and Balderstone are outstanding for the visitors while Liverpool keeper Clemence is a virtual spectator as the Carlisle defence shows resilience and determination.

			Att	F-A	H-T	Scorers, Times, and Referees	1	2	3	4	5	6	7	8	9	10	11	12 sub used
4R	H	LIVERPOOL 4 W	21,262 1:2	0:2	0:0	Boersma 50, Toshack 81; Ref: J Taylor	Ross	Carr	Gorman	O'Neill	Green	Balderstone	Martin	Train*	Owen	Clarke F	Laidlaw	Tiler
						Clemence	*Smith*	*Lindsay*	*Thompson*	*Lloyd*	*Hughes*	*Keegan*	*Hall*	*Boersma*	*Toshack*	*Callaghan*	

In a more even first half, Carlisle take the game to their opponents and Clemence makes a fine save from O'Neill. Boersma finally breaks the deadlock from Keegan's opening. O'Neill hits the post with a neat shot before Toshack wraps up the result following Hall's clever dribble.

Home and Away record

	P		Home						Away				Pts
		W	D	L	F	A	W	D	L	F	A	
1 Middlesbro'	42	16	4	1	40	8	11	7	3	37	22	65
2 Luton T	42	12	5	4	42	25	7	7	7	22	26	50
3 CARLISLE U	42	13	5	3	40	17	7	4	10	21	31	49
4 Orient	42	9	8	4	28	17	6	10	5	27	25	48
5 Blackpool	42	11	5	5	35	17	6	8	7	22	23	47
6 Sunderland	42	11	6	4	32	15	8	3	10	26	29	47
7 Nottingham F	42	12	6	3	40	19	3	9	9	17	24	45
8 West Brom	42	8	9	4	28	24	6	7	8	20	21	44
9 Hull C	42	9	9	3	25	15	4	8	9	21	32	43
10 Notts Co	42	8	6	7	30	35	4	7	7	25	25	43
11 Bolton W	42	12	5	4	30	17	3	7	11	14	23	42
12 Millwall	42	10	6	5	28	16	4	8	9	23	35	42
13 Fulham	42	11	4	6	26	20	5	6	10	13	23	42
14 Aston Villa	42	8	9	4	33	21	5	6	10	15	24	41
15 Portsmouth	42	9	8	4	26	16	5	4	12	19	46	40
16 Bristol C	42	9	5	7	25	20	5	5	11	22	34	38
17 Cardiff C	42	8	7	6	27	20	2	9	10	22	42	36
18 Oxford U	42	8	8	5	27	21	2	8	11	8	25	36
19 Sheffield W	42	9	6	6	33	24	3	5	13	18	39	35
20 Crystal Pal	42	6	7	8	24	24	5	5	11	19	32	34
21 Preston N E*	42	7	8	6	24	23	2	6	13	16	39	31
22 Swindon T	42	6	7	8	22	27	1	4	16	14	45	25
	924	212	143	107	665	441	107	143	212	441	665	923

* one point deducted

Odds & ends

Double wins: (5) Notts Co, Oxford U, Crystal P, Fulham, Orient.
Double defeats: (2) Portsmouth, Blackpool.

Won from behind: (3) Oxford (h), Millwall (a), Nottingham F (h).
Lost from in front: (1) Sunderland (a).

High spots: Beating Orient 3-0 in front of the Match of the Day cameras. Gaining promotion with perfect timing, reaching a top-three spot in the last game of the season.
Beating Sunderland before the biggest home League gate for 23 years.
Knocking holders Sunderland out of the FA Cup.
Holding Liverpool at Anfield in the FA Cup.
Winning the second half at Luton.
Low spots: Losing 1-6 at Luton and being 0-6 down after 34 minutes.

Ever presents: (1) Joe Laidlaw.
Hat-tricks: (1) Frank Clarke (4 goals) v Swindon (h).
Opposing hat-tricks: None.
Leading scorer: Frank Clark (16).

Appearances and Goals

	Appearances						Goals			
	Lge	*Sub*	LC	*Sub*	FAC	*Sub*	Lge	LC	FAC	Tot
Balderstone, Chris	26	2	2		3	1	1	1		2
Barry, Mike	9	1	1	1						
Carr, Peter	37		4		3					
Clarke, Frank	36		3		4		16			16
Clarke, Tom	1									
Delgado, Bob	2	3		1	1	1				
Gorman, John	37		4		4					
Green, Bill	40		4		4		2			2
Laidlaw, Joe	42		4		4		12			12
Martin, Dennis	41		4		4		7	1	1	9
McCartney, Mike	1	3								
O'Neill, Les	37		3		4		6	1		7
Owen, Bobby	36	2	4		4		11	2		13
Ross, Allan	41		4		4					
Ternent, Stan	13		1							
Tiler, Brian	22		3		1	1	3			3
Train, Ray	26	1	1		4		1			1
Winstanley, Graham	15	1	1		1		2			2
(own-goals)										
18 players used	462	13	44	2	44	2	61	5	1	67

LEAGUE DIVISION 1

Manager: Alan Ashman

SEASON 1974-75

Fixtures

No	Venue	Opponent	Date	Att	Pos	Result	Pt	F-A	H-T	Scorers, Times	Referee
1	A	CHELSEA	17/8	31,268 (20)	4	W	2	2-0	1-0	Green 2, O'Neill 75	P Reeves
2	A	MIDDLESBROUGH	20/8	28,719 (10)	1	W	4	2-0	1-0	O'Neill 14, 52	M Lowe
3	H	TOTTENHAM	24/8	18,426 (22)	1	W	6	1-0	1-0	Balderstone 20p	R Capey
4	H	MIDDLESBROUGH	27/8	18,473 (6)	3	L	6	0-1	0-1	Armstrong 2	I Smith
5	A	LEICESTER C	31/8	20,658 (15)	5	D	7	1-1	1-0	McIlmoyle 10, Worthington 85p	A James
6	H	STOKE C	7/9	14,507 (4)	7	L	7	0-2	0-1	Hudson 6, Ritchie 58	E Garner
7	A	NEWCASTLE U	14/9	40,544 (8)	9	L	7	0-1	0-0	Tudor 88	R Lee
8	H	BIRMINGHAM C	21/9	12,691 (18)	9	W	9	1-0	0-0	O'Neill 56	P Willis
9	H	MANCHESTER C	24/9	17,495 (3)	8	D	10	0-0	0-0		L Hayes
10	A	LUTON T	28/9	12,987 (17)	11	L	10	1-3	1-1	Laidlaw 37 / Anderson 13, Alston 54, Ryan Jim 76p	J Homewood

Line-ups

No	Team	1	2	3	4	5	6	7	8	9	10	11	12 sub used
1	Carlisle	Ross	Carr	Gorman	O'Neill	Green	Parker	McIlmoyle	Train	Clarke F*	Balderstone	Laidlaw	Martin
1	Chelsea	Bonetti	Locke	Houseman	Hollins	Droy	Harris	Kember	Hay	Garland	Garner*	Sissons	Cooke
2	Carlisle	Ross	Platt	Gorman*	O'Neill	Green	Parker	Martin	Train	McIlmoyle	Balderstone	Laidlaw	Clarke F
2	Middlesbrough	Platt	Craggs	Spraggon	Souness	Boam	Maddren	Murdoch	Mills	Hickton*	Foggon	Armstrong	Smith
3	Carlisle	Ross	Carr	Winstanley	O'Neill	Green	Parker	Martin	Train	McIlmoyle*	Balderstone	Laidlaw	Clarke F
3	Tottenham	Jennings	Evans	Naylor	Beal	England	Coates	Pratt	Perryman	Jones*	Peters	Neighbour	McGrath
4	Carlisle	Ross	Platt	Gorman	O'Neill	Green	Parker	Martin	Train	McIlmoyle	Balderstone	Laidlaw	
4	Middlesbrough	Platt	Craggs	Spraggon	Souness	Boam	Maddren	Murdoch	Mills	Hickton	Foggon	Armstrong	
5	Carlisle	Ross	Carr	Gorman	O'Neill	Green	Parker	Martin	Train	McIlmoyle	Balderstone	Laidlaw	Waters
5	Leicester C	Wallington	Whitworth	Rofe	Sammels	Munro	Cross	Weller	Earle*	Worthington	Birchenall	Glover	
6	Carlisle	Ross	Carr	Gorman	O'Neill	Green	Parker	Barry*	Train	McIlmoyle	Balderstone	Laidlaw	Owen
6	Stoke C	Farmer	Marsh	Pejic	Mahoney	Smith	Dodd	Haslegrave	Greenhoff	Ritchie	Hudson	Salmons	
7	Carlisle	Ross	Carr	Gorman	O'Neill	Green	Parker	Clarke F	Train	McIlmoyle	Balderstone	Laidlaw	Owen
7	Newcastle U	McFaul	Nattrass	Clark	McDermott*	Keeley	Howard	Burns	Cassidy	MacDonald	Tudor	Hibbitt	Smith
8	Carlisle	Ross	Carr	Gorman	O'Neill	Green	Parker	Clarke F	Train	McIlmoyle	Balderstone	Laidlaw	Roberts
8	Birmingham C	Latchford	Martin*	Styles!	Kendall	Gallagher	Page	Campbell	Francis	Burns	Hatton	Taylor	
9	Carlisle	Ross	Carr	Gorman	O'Neill	Green	Parker	Martin	Train	McIlmoyle	Balderstone	Laidlaw	Henson
9	Manchester C	MacRae	Hammond	Donachie	Doyle*	Barrett	Oakes	Summerbee	Bell	Marsh	Hartford	Tueart	
10	Carlisle	Ross	Carr	Gorman	O'Neill	Green	Parker	Martin	Train	McIlmoyle	Balderstone	Laidlaw	
10	Luton T	Barber	Shanks	Thomson	Anderson	Faulkner	Ryan John	Hindson	Ryan Jimmy	Husband	West	Alston	

Match reports

1. Chelsea — One of the most famous games in the club's history begins with Bill Green's close-range goal, the fastest in the whole of the Football League. Chelsea come back to hit the woodwork twice and put Carlisle under pressure. Les O'Neill's cross cum shot puts the issue beyond doubt.

2. Middlesbrough — O'Neill gives United the lead with a well-placed shot after a neat pass from Laidlaw. An unstoppable glancing header gives him his second after a long Carlisle build up ends with Carr's cross. Carlisle stay in control, although Maddren nearly pulls one goal back late in the game.

3. Tottenham — United's penalty comes after England up-ends Laidlaw. After his first effort was saved when Jennings moved, Balderstone crashes home the retake. Train hits the bar from 35 yards and though Tottenham come into the game more after half-time Carlisle are never in any real danger.

4. Middlesbrough — Carlisle drop their first points and concede their first goal when Armstrong's early strike from 18 yards surprises the home side. Carlisle are frustrated by the Boro defence though O'Neill comes close to scoring. McIlmoyle's missed half-volley late on sums up Carlisle's frustration.

5. Leicester C — McIlmoyle's neat finish against his old club puts Carlisle in the lead. Cross fouls Laidlaw but Balderstone misses the spot-kick. The Foxes come into the game more but Carlisle hold firm till Carr is judged to have brought down Glover. Worthington easily converts the penalty.

6. Stoke C — Hudson puts the visitors ahead with a neat shot after the Carlisle defence has been carved open by the visitors. Stoke stay in control and Ritchie makes it two with a bustling effort after Greenhoff's shot is part saved. Pejic then raps hard against the crossbar as Carlisle finish second best.

7. Newcastle U — The Magpies take the game to Carlisle as the United rearguard is tested and Ross earns his corn with some fine saves. Carlisle come into the game more after the interval but finally substitute Smith finds his way to the bye-line and Tudor hits an unstoppable shot from his neat pass.

8. Birmingham C — Carlisle took the likelier to score in the first half, though there are chances for both teams. McIlmoyle is brought down in the area and O'Neill scores after Balderstone's penalty is parried. Styles is sent off for arguing but Carlisle cannot make their numerical advantage count further.

9. Manchester C — Despite the scoreline, this game sees one of Carlisle's more authoritative performances. McIlmoyle, Green and Laidlaw all go close before the break and soon after Train's effort is chalked off for offside. City come more into the match and a Bell header hits the outside of the post.

10. Luton T — Anderson scores from Alston's defence-splitting pass but the lively Laidlaw equalises with an overhead kick from a McIlmoyle knock down. Alston then puts the home side ahead after a dribble through the United defence before Jimmy Ryan's spot-kick after Parker handles the ball.

Carlisle United — 1974/75 season match record (matches 11–21)

11 — H LIVERPOOL, 5/10
Att 20,844 · Pos 13 · 2 · 10 · 0-1 L · 0-1 · 0-1
Scorer: Kennedy 36
Ref: J Hunting

Ross	Carr	Gorman	O'Neill	Green	Parker	Martin	Train	McIlmoyle	Owen	Laidlaw	
Clemence	*Smith*	*Lindsay*	*Lawler*	*Boersma*	*Hughes*	*Keegan*	*Hall*	*Heighway*	*Kennedy**	*Callaghan*	*Cormack*

Keegan returns after his eight week suspension but has a quiet game as both sides seek early advantage. Boersma's clever jinking run ends with Kennedy hitting home for the game's only goal. Carlisle continue to play neat football but are punished for one moment of lost concentration.

12 — A WOLVERHAMPTON, 12/10
Att 18,918 · Pos 15 · 10 · 10 · 0-2 L · 0-2 · 0-1
Scorers: Withe 26, Parkin 76
Ref: A Grey

Clarke T	Carr	Gorman	Balderstone	Green	Parker	Martin	Train	Clarke F	Owen	Barry	
Pierce	*Palmer*	*Parkin*	*Bailey*	*Jefferson*	*McAlle*	*Hibbitt**	*Daley*	*Richards*	*Dougan*	*Sunderland*	*Withe*

Parkin's cross finds Dougan who heads on for Withe to score acrobatically. Clarke's header unluckily hits the post but Wolves dominate after the interval. Parkin shoots home from 30 yards to seal it for the home side, though Clarke should have reduced the arrears from Owen's cross.

13 — A TOTTENHAM H, 16/10
Att 12,823 · Pos 14 · 22 · 11 · 1-1 D · 1-1 · 1-1
Scorers: Owen 5, Chivers 44
Ref: K Baker

Ross	Carr	Gorman	Balderstone	Green	Parker	Martin	Train	Clarke F	Owen	Barry	
Jennings	*Evans*	*Knowles*	*Pratt*	*England*	*Naylor*	*Perryman*	*Neighbour*	*Chivers*	*Jones*	*Coates*	

Owen silences the meagre crowd by sweeping home Barry's cross. Chivers is the main threat from bottom of the table Spurs and he heads in from Naylor's flick on. Both sides go close after the break, never more so than Chivers' free header late on that Ross holds to save a point.

14 — H DERBY CO, 19/10
Att 13,353 · Pos 14 · 7 · 13 · 3-0 W · 3-0 · 1-0
Scorers: Train 42, Martin 66, Clarke F 70
Ref: B Matthewson

Clarke T	Carr	Gorman	Balderstone	Green	Parker	Martin	Train	McIlmoyle	Owen	Barry	
Boulton	*Webster*	*Nish*	*Rioch*	*Daniel*	*Todd*	*Newton*	*Gemmill*	*Davies*	*Hector*	*Lee*	

Somewhat against the run of play, Train's angled shot puts Carlisle into the lead following work by Martin and Balderstone. Martin scores the second after Clarke's effort rebounds back off the post. Carlisle are now very much on top and Clarke taps in the third after a defensive mix up.

15 — A COVENTRY C, 26/10
Att 17,070 · Pos 15 · 14 · 13 · 1-2 L · 1-2 · 0-1
Scorers: Clarke F 20, Lloyd 15, 63
Ref: M Sinclair

Clarke T	Carr	Gorman	Barry	Green	Parker	Martin	Train	Clarke F*	Owen	Balderstone	McIlmoyle
Ramsbottom	*Oakey*	*Cattlin*	*Mortimer*	*Lloyd*	*Hindley*	*Holmes*	*Craven*	*Stein*	*Cross**	*Hutchison*	*Alderson*

Centre-half Lloyd uses his height to good effect to flick Cattlin's shot into the net for the first goal. Clarke nets after Ramsbottom fails to hold the ball. Lloyd heads in again from Mortimer's corner-kick and, although Carlisle press for an equaliser, Lloyd is equally effective in defence.

16 — A SHEFFIELD U, 2/11
Att 17,679 · Pos 17 · 8 · 13 · 1-2 L · 1-2 · 1-2
Scorers: McIlmoyle 23, Field 15, 17
Ref: E Jolly

Clarke T	Carr	Gorman	Balderstone	Green	Parker	Martin	Train	McIlmoyle	Clarke F	Barry	
Brown	*Badger*	*Hemsley*	*Garbutt**	*Colquhoun*	*Eddy*	*Woodward*	*Speight*	*Dearden*	*Currie*	*Field*	*Bradford*

Clarke fails to hold Dearden's centre and Field scores easily. He scores again two minutes later from an Eddy through ball before a trademark McIlmoyle header from Carr's long cross reduces the deficit. Carlisle come more into the game after half-time, but the Blades just hold out.

17 — H WEST HAM U, 9/11
Att 14,141 · Pos 17 · 9 · 13 · 0-1 L · 0-1 · 0-0
Ref: K Styles

Clarke T	Carr	Gorman	O'Neill	Green	Parker	Martin	Train	Clarke F	McIlmoyle	Balderstone	
Day	*Coleman*	*Lampard*	*Bonds*	*Taylor T*	*Lock*	*Jennings*	*Paddon*	*Gould*	*Brooking*	*Robson*	

Carlisle, with the wind behind them fail to take advantage on a heavy pitch. The visitors, and Brooking in particular, master the conditions better and Lampard scores from 20 yards following Robson's flick on. Clarke hits the post in the last minute as Carlisle continue to press hard.

18 — A QP RANGERS, 16/11
Att 15,700 · Pos 21 · 15 · 13 · 1-2 L · 1-2 · 0-2
Scorers: Parker 54p, Thomas 28, Bowles 41
Ref: R Kirkpatrick

Ross	Carr	Gorman	O'Neill	Green	Parker	Martin	Train	Laidlaw*	Clarke F	Balderstone	Owen
Parkes	*Hazell*	*Gillard*	*Leach*	*McLintock*	*Clement*	*Thomas*	*Francis*	*Rogers*	*Bowles*	*Givens*	

Bowles, Thomas and Francis are controlling the game for QPR and Thomas nets from Gillard's through ball. Bowles gets the second against his old club as Givens' shot is not cleared. Parker scores from the spot after O'Neill is upended by Clement but QPR are deserved winners.

19 — H LEEDS U, 23/11
Att 19,975 · Pos 21 · 16 · 13 · 1-2 L · 1-2 · 1-0
Scorers: Martin 7, Jordan 47, McKenzie 85
Ref: D Wallace

Ross	Carr	Gorman	O'Neill	Green	Parker	Martin	Train	Clarke F	Prudham*	Laidlaw	Barry
Harvey	*Reaney*	*Cherry*	*Bremner*	*McQueen*	*Madeley*	*McKenzie*	*Clarke*	*Jordan*	*Giles*	*Yorath*	

Martin's early strike from 20 yards after debutant Prudham dispossesses McQueen puts Carlisle in the driving seat till half-time. Leeds survive going further behind and Jordan's blind side header brings them level. McKenzie slots home as Carlisle's defence briefly loses concentration.

20 — A IPSWICH T, 30/11
Att 20,122 · Pos 21 · 2 · 13 · 1-3 L · 1-3 · 0-2
Scorers: O'Neill 54, Hamilton 2, Johnson 21, Lambert 82
Ref: T Spencer

Ross	Carr	Gorman	O'Neill	Green	Parker	Martin	Train*	Clarke F	Prudham	Laidlaw	
Sivell	*Mills*	*Harper*	*Talbot*	*Peddelty*	*Beattie*	*Hamilton*	*Viljoen*	*Johnson*	*Whymark**	*Woods*	*Lambert*

Ipswich start well and already have a goal disallowed before Hamilton's low shot finds the net. Johnson scores from the edge of the area as Town are in control. O'Neill's fine 20-yard strike gives Carlisle hope after the break but Mills' long pass puts Lambert clear for the final goal.

21 — H ARSENAL, 7/12
Att 12,926 · Pos 20 · 18 · 15 · 2-1 W · 2-1 · 1-0
Scorers: Prudham 14, Martin 65, Kidd 79
Ref: E Garner

Ross	Carr	Gorman	O'Neill	Green	Parker	Martin	Train	Clarke F	Prudham	Barry	
Rimmer	*Rice*	*McNab*	*Kelly*	*Simpson*	*Mancini*	*Storey*	*Ball*	*Radford*	*Kidd*	*Cropley*	

Cropley makes his Arsenal debut but Prudham nods the home side ahead from Gorman's cross. Despite vigorous Arsenal tackling, Carlisle dominate and Martin's individual effort produces the second just before a brawl breaks out. Kidd pulls one back from Simpson's through ball.

LEAGUE DIVISION 1

Manager: Alan Ashman **SEASON 1974-75**

No / Venue & Opp	Date	Att	Pos	Pt	F-A	H-T	Scorers, Times, and Referees	1	2	3	4	5	6	7	8	9	10	11	12 sub used
22 H CHELSEA	14/12	12,854	21	15	L 1-2	1-2	Martin 13	Ross	Carr	Gorman	O'Neill	Green	Parker	Martin	Train	Clarke F	Prudham*	Barry	Balderstone
			18				Hollins 3, 22 — Ref: J Williams	Phillips	Locke	Harris	Hollins	Droy	Hay	Kember	Wilkins	Garland	Hutchinson	Cooke	
23 A EVERTON	21/12	33,489	20	17	W 3-2	0-1	Laidlaw 53, 57, O'Neill 64	Ross	Carr	Gorman	O'Neill	Green	Parker	Martin	Train	Clarke F*	Laidlaw	Balderstone	McIlmoyle
			2				Latchford 6, 51 — Ref: I Jones	Davies	Bernard	Seargeant	Clemens	Kenyon	Hurst	Jones	Telfer*	Latchford	Lyons	Connolly	Buckley
24 H NEWCASTLE U	26/12	20,675	20	17	L 1-2	0-1	Owen 76	Ross	Carr	Gorman	O'Neill	Green	Parker	Martin	Train	McIlmoyle*	Laidlaw	Balderstone	Owen
			9				Tudor 27, MacDonald 90 — Ref: M Lowe	McFaul	Nattrass	Kennedy	Smith	Keeley	Howard	Barrowc'gh	Nulty	MacDonald	Tudor	Craig	
25 A BURNLEY	28/12	19,382	20	17	L 1-2	1-0	Martin 16	Ross	Carr	McCartney	O'Neill	Green	Parker	Martin	Train	Owen	Laidlaw	Balderstone	
			7				James 50, Collins 89 — Ref: R Perkin	Stevenson	Newton	Brennan	Ingham	Waldron	Flynn	Noble	Hankin	Fletcher	Collins	James	
26 A ARSENAL	11/1	21,538	20	17	L 1-2	1-1	O'Neill 36	Ross	Parker	Spearritt	O'Neill	Green	Balderstone	Barry	Train	Owen	Laidlaw	Clarke F	
			18				Radford 30, Cropley 89 — Ref: K Burns	Rimmer	Rice	McNab	Kelly	Mancini	Simpson	Armstrong	Ball	Radford	Kidd	Cropley	
27 H IPSWICH T	18/1	13,054	20	19	W 2-1	1-1	Clarke F 24, Laidlaw 51	Ross	Spearritt	Gorman	O'Neill	Green	Parker	Martin	Train	Owen	Laidlaw	Clarke F	
			2				Whymark 35 — Ref: D Richardson	Sivell	Burley	Mills	Talbot	Hunter	Beattie	Osborne*	Viljoen	Johnson	Whymark	Lambert	Woods
28 A WEST HAM U	1/2	26,805	20	19	L 0-2	0-2		Ross	Spearritt	Gorman	O'Neill	Green	Parker	Martin*	Train	Owen	Laidlaw	Clarke F	Barry
			6				Jennings 19, Holland 39 — Ref: R Crabb	Day	McDowall	Lampard	Bonds	Taylor T	Lock	Jennings	Paddon	Robson	Brooking*	Holland	Best
29 H SHEFFIELD U	8/2	12,023	20	19	L 0-1	0-1		Ross	Carr	Spearritt	O'Neill	Green	Parker	Martin	Train	Owen	Laidlaw	Clarke F*	McIlmoyle
			11				Jones 28 — Ref: B Matthewson	Brown	Badger	Hemsley	Eddy	Colquhoun	Flynn*	Woodward	Speight	Jones	Currie	Field	Dearden
30 H QP RANGERS	22/2	13,176	22	19	L 1-2	1-1	Owen 17	Ross	Carr	Spearritt	O'Neill	Green	Parker	Martin	Train	Owen	Laidlaw	Clarke F	
			13				Givens 12, 72 — Ref: H Davey	Parkes	Shanks	Gillard	Masson*	McLintock	Clement	Thomas	Rogers	Back	Bowles	Givens	Busby
31 A LEEDS U	25/2	32,346	22	19	L 1-3	0-1	Laidlaw 74	Ross	Carr	Spearritt	O'Neill	Green	Parker	Martin*	Train	Owen	Laidlaw	Clarke F	Balderstone
			6				Lorimer 28, Clarke 65, Gray E 73 — Ref: B Homewood	Stewart	Reaney	Gray F	Bremner	Hunter	Madeley	Lorimer	Clarke	Jordan	Giles	Gray E	

22 — H CHELSEA: Fellow relegation candidates Chelsea take the lead when Hollins chips a simple goal. Martin strikes a fine equaliser from the edge of the area after a corner-kick was not cleared, but Hollins hits his second after Green failed to clear. An injury to Prudham mars the goalless second half.

23 — A EVERTON: Latchford's two goals look to have put the game beyond the visitors' reach. Laidlaw pulls one back by heading in Carr's centre and scores again when he meets Davies' clearance to stroke the ball home. O'Neill completes the fairytale by heading home Balderstone's perfect cross.

24 — H NEWCASTLE U: Carlisle make the early running but it is the visitors who score first when Tudor heads in Barrowclough's cross. Newcastle continue to look the more dangerous but Owen seizes on a poor Nattrass back-pass to level. MacDonald surges through in the last minute to steal a painful victory.

25 — A BURNLEY: Martin's chip shot puts Carlisle ahead after Stevenson is caught off his line. Burnley find another gear after half-time and James scores with a curling shot. In almost the last minute Collins shoots following a long throw, and although his first effort is blocked, he nets from the rebound.

26 — A ARSENAL: With both sides desperate for points, Radford's left-foot strike from Armstrong's centre draws first blood. O'Neill heads in Owen's chipped pass to equalise. Carlisle's makeshift defence holds out till the last minute when, after an inswinging corner-kick, Cropley stabs the ball home.

27 — H IPSWICH T: League leaders Ipswich dominate early on but ex Town star Clarke scores from close range. Whymark heads in Viljoen's free-kick for the equaliser. Laidlaw scores the winner from 20 yards before Lambert hits the woodwork. Parker and O'Neill both miss a twice-taken penalty.

28 — A WEST HAM U: The Hammers take the lead when Ross misses Lock's free-kick and Jennings nets from an acute angle. Carlisle strive to get on level terms but O'Neill's back-pass sells Ross short and Holland accepts the gift. The Londoners adapt to the wet conditions better though Owen hits the post.

29 — H SHEFFIELD U: Carlisle take the game to the visitors and Spearritt's shot grazes the bar. A defensive blunder sets up Gary Jones to score from Currie's pass. After the break Carlisle strive to equalise and Brown makes some fine saves. The Blades seldom threaten but are content to contain Carlisle.

30 — H QP RANGERS: The visitors start positively and Givens heads home from a Thomas corner. Clarke misses before Owen's header from an O'Neill centre beats Parkes. After the break Carlisle throw everything into attack but Givens nods in from a Thomas cross to settle the game as QPR play out time.

31 — A LEEDS U: Peter Lorimer's trademark 25-yard drive gives Ross no chance. Carlisle fight back before Clarke's goal, set up by Bremner and Lorimer, rocks the Cumbrians. Gray, who torments the visitors all evening, gets the third. Laidlaw hits a fine solo goal, the first Leeds concede in eight games.

32 · H · 1/3 · LEICESTER C · L 0-1 · 22 · 20 · 19 · 12,676

Ross	Carr	Spearritt	O'Neill	Green	Parker	Martin	Train	Owen	Laidlaw	Clarke F*	Gorman
Wallington	Whitworth	Rofe	Lee	Blockley	Cross	Weller	Sammels	Worthington	Birchenall	Glover	

Worthington 68
Ref: L. Hayes

Carlisle have more possession in the first half but cannot make their dominance count. Leicester come out of their shell after the interval and Spearritt heads Glover's shot off the line but Lee sets up Worthington for a decisive finish. Ross makes two saves as the Foxes stay in control.

33 · H · 15/3 · LUTON T · L 1-2 · 22 · 21 · 19 · 8,339

Ross	Carr	Gorman	O'Neill	Green	Parker	Martin	Train	Owen	Laidlaw	Clarke F*	McIlmoyle
Barber	Ryan John	Buckley	Anderson	Faulkner	Futcher P	Ryan Jimmy	Husband	Futcher R	West	Aston*	Alston

Laidlaw 55 / Alston 60, Futcher R 87
Ref: J Rice

Before a sparse crowd McIlmoyle hits the bar before Anderson and Alston threaten for Luton. From Martin's cross Laidlaw heads the opening goal but Alston replies after Husband's effort rebounds to him. Futcher's long centre-cum-cross drifts in off the goalpost to sink poor Carlisle.

34 · A · 19/3 · MANCHESTER C · W 2-1 · 22 · 12 · 21 · 24,047

Ross	Carr	Spearritt	O'Neill	Green	Parker	Martin	Train	Owen	Laidlaw	Clarke F
Corrigan	Doyle	Donachie	Hartford	Clarke	Oates	Summerbee*	Bell	Royle	Barnes	Tueart	Keegan

Laidlaw 23, 39 / Barnes
Ref: J Taylor

Laidlaw opens the scoring with a superb volley from the edge of the area that catches Corrigan off his line. Barnes equalises with a left-foot drive from Summerbee's pass for his first senior goal. Laidlaw's lob gives Carlisle both points, ending an awful run of six consecutive defeats.

35 · A · 22/3 · STOKE C · L 2-5 · 22 · 5 · 21 · 20,545

Ross	Carr	Spearritt	O'Neill	Green	Parker	Martin	Train	Owen	Laidlaw	Clarke F	Balderstone
Shilton	Marsh	Mahoney	Dodd	Skeels	Conroy	Greenhoff	Hurst*	Hudson	Salmons	Moores	

Laidlaw 18, Carr 78 (Salmons 88) / Conroy 7, 65, 72, Greenhoff 68,
Ref: R Tinkler

Terry Conroy scores from close range but Laidlaw nets from Owen's knock down in an even first half. Conroy converts Salmons' centre before Greenhoff heads in. After Conroy clinches his hat-trick, Carr's header reduces the deficit, before Stoke go nap through star man Salmons.

36 · A · 25/3 · BIRMINGHAM C · L 0-2 · 22 · 13 · 21 · 33,761

Ross	Carr	Spearritt	O'Neill*	Green	Parker	Martin	Train	Owen*	Laidlaw	Clarke F	Balderstone
Sprake	Calderwood Bryant	Pendrey	Gallagher	Roberts	Campbell	Francis	Burns	Hatton	Taylor		

Francis 40, Burns 86
Ref: J Bent

In an ill-tempered game, Sprake and Owen are stretchered off though Spake later returns. Francis scores from 30 yards having also struck the woodwork. Carlisle dominate the second half but cannot break through and Burns finishes from close range after Hatton's effort hits the bar.

37 · H · 29/3 · EVERTON · W 3-0 · 22 · 2 · 23 · 16,049

Clarke T	Carr	Gorman	Clements*	Green	Parker	Martin	Train	Balderstone*	Laidlaw	Clarke F	McCartney
Davies	Scott	Seageant	Kenyon	Hurst	Buckley	Dobson	Lyons	Latchford	Jones	Pearson	

Laidlaw 63p, Martin 80, Clarke F 87
Ref: P Willis

Following an even first period, United take control after the break with Laidlaw's twice-taken penalty after Scott brings down Martin. Martin himself scores the second with a perfect chip from Carr's short free-kick. Clarke wraps it up with a decisive header after Train has centred.

38 · H · 1/4 · BURNLEY · W 4-2 · 22 · 7 · 25 · 12,793

Clarke T	Carr	Gorman	O'Neill*	Green	Parker	Martin	Train	Balderstone	Laidlaw	Clarke F*	Spearritt
Finn	Newton	Brennan	Noble	Waldron	Dixey	Flynn	Hankin	Ingham	Parker	James	

O'Neill 26, Laidlaw 37p, 90, Train 88 / Parker 38, James 59p
Ref: J Yates

In a classic encounter, United go two up through O'Neill's strike and Laidlaw's spot-kick after Train is fouled. Parker's 25-yarder and James' penalty after Green brings down Brennan make it all square. Train hits a spectacular winner before Laidlaw's effort seals it for the home side.

39 · H · 5/4 · COVENTRY C · D 0-0 · 21 · 2 · 26 · 10,857

Clarke T	Carr	Gorman	Owen	Green	Parker	Martin	Train	Balderstone	Laidlaw	Clarke F*	Prudham
Ramsbottom Coop	Cattlin	Craven	Lloyd	Dugdale	Oakey	Mortimer	Cross	Green	Hutchison		

Ref: A Porter

Following an even first period, United take control after the break. In one of the season's duller encounters Prudham has a goal disallowed soon after replacing the injured Clarke. Balderstone's effort is blocked on the line but Coventry's rugged defence stifles Carlisle's neat approach work. Clarke's only real save comes from a bad Gorman back-pass.

40 · A · 12/4 · LIVERPOOL · L 0-2 · 22 · 2 · 26 · 46,073

Clarke T	Carr	Gorman	O'Neill	Green	Parker	Martin	Train	Balderstone	Laidlaw	Clarke F*	Owen
Clemence	Smith	Neal	Thompson	Cormack	Hughes	Keegan	Hall	Kennedy	Toshack	Callaghan	

Toshack 65, Keegan 75
Ref: K Styles

United are relegated after this defeat but at half-time Balderstone nearly puts Carlisle ahead. Toshack breaks the deadlock getting a touch to Neal's corner and the visitors' last hopes are extinguished when Keegan hits home a loose ball after Carr blocks Kennedy's effort on the line.

41 · H · 19/4 · WOLVERHAMPTON · W 1-0 · 22 · 13 · 28 · 9,707

Ross	Carr	Spearritt	O'Neill	Green	Parker	Martin	Train	Prudham	Laidlaw	Balderstone
Pierce	Palmer	Parkin	Bailey	Jefferson	McAlle	Hibbitt	Carr	Withe*	Kindon	Farley	Daley

Martin 38
Ref: J Williams

The visitors begin brightly and Hibbitt twice comes close to scoring. Carlisle respond with a shot by O'Neill that is blocked before Martin scores from the rebound. The second half sees Carlisle hold their lead as Kindon's effort is ruled offside. Pierce denies Laidlaw late on.

42 · A · 26/4 · DERBY CO · D 0-0 · 22 · 1 · 29 · 38,000

Ross	Carr	Spearritt	O'Neill	Green	Parker	Martin	Train	Clarke F	Laidlaw	Balderstone
Boulton	Thomas	Nish	Rioch	McFarland	Todd	Newton	Gemmill	Davies	Hector	Lee*	Hinton

Ref: R Morrissey

A capacity crowd watches Derby presented with the championship trophy as Carlisle's season in Division One comes to an end. On a sunny day it is a game of few chances though Hinton's entry off the bench livens up the proceedings. At the end honour is satisfied for both teams.

Home 14,525 · Away 25,356 · Average

LEAGUE DIVISION 1 (CUP-TIES)

Manager: Alan Ashman

League Cup

2 A BRADFORD C — 11/9 — 7 W — Att 6,969 4:4 — F-A 1-0 — H-T 1-0
Scorers: O'Neill 38 — Ref: G Hill

1	2	3	4	5	6	7	8	9	10	11	12 sub used
Ross	Carr	Gorman	O'Neill	Green	Parker	Clarke F	Train	McIlmoyle	Balderstone	Laidlaw	
Downsboro'	*Podd*	*Cooper*	*Cooke*	*Napier*	*Fretwell*	*Brown*	*Ham*	*Ingram*	*Johnson*	*Hutchins*	

The home side takes the game to Carlisle to try and hustle them out of their stride but, minutes after Laidlaw hits the post, O'Neill bundles the ball home against his old club. City continue to press but their aerial bombardment poses little real threat to Green and his fellow defenders.

3 A COLCHESTER U — 9/10 — 13 L — Att 7,842 3:3 — F-A 0-2 — H-T 0-0
Scorers: Svarc 77, Leslie 80p — Ref: P Reeves

1	2	3	4	5	6	7	8	9	10	11	12 sub used
Clarke T	Carr	Gorman	Winstanley	Green	Parker	Martin	Train	Clarke F	Owen	Spearritt	Smith L
Walker	*Smith A*	*Packer*	*Leslie*	*Morgan**	*Harford*	*Thomas*	*Svarc*	*Froggatt*	*Lindsay*	*Cook*	

Carlisle's tidy football looks to be enough to ease them past their opponents but Martin's poor back-pass is intercepted by Svarc who puts the Us ahead. Three minutes later Carr is controversially judged to be guilty of holding and Leslie efficiently despatches the resulting penalty.

FA Cup

3 A PRESTON N E — 4/1 — 20 W — Att 18,682 3:7 — F-A 1-0 — H-T 1-0
Scorers: Laidlaw 29 — Ref: J Hunting

1	2	3	4	5	6	7	8	9	10	11	12 sub used
Ross	Carr	Gorman	O'Neill	Green	Parker	Barry	Train	Owen	Laidlaw	Balderstone	
Tunks	*Fielding*	*Burns*	*Doyle*	*Bird*	*Sadler*	*Lamb*	*Morley*	*Elwiss*	*Holden*	*Charlton*	

Preston have more of the early play but Laidlaw puts Carlisle ahead with an opportunist effort after O'Neill's strike is blocked. After the break, United survive a penalty appeal as the home side continues to dominate. Ross in goal is outstanding as Carlisle's defence somehow holds firm.

4 H WEST BROMWICH — 25/1 — 20 W — Att 14,843 2:5 — F-A 3-2 — H-T 2-1
Scorers: Clarke F 10, Laidlaw 30, Owen 61; Brown 26p, Nisbet 70 — Ref: H Hackney

1	2	3	4	5	6	7	8	9	10	11	12 sub used
Ross	Spearritt	Gorman	O'Neill	Green	Parker	Martin	Train	Owen	Laidlaw	Clarke F	
Osborne	*Nisbet*	*Wilson*	*Cantello*	*Wile*	*Rushbury*	*Brown*	*Shaw*	*Mayo*	*Hughes*	*Johnston*	

On a sodden pitch, both sides combine to produce a classic Cup-tie. Clarke gives Carlisle the lead from 12 yards but West Brom equalise when Train concedes a spot kick. Laidlaw with a low shot and Owen put Carlisle ahead but Nisbet pulls one back after a crazy goalmouth scramble.

5 A MANSFIELD T — 15/2 — 20 W — Att 18,293 4:1 — F-A 1-0 — H-T 1-0
Scorers: Owen 21 — Ref: J Taylor

1	2	3	4	5	6	7	8	9	10	11	12 sub used
Ross	Spearritt	Gorman	O'Neill	Green	Parker	Martin	Train	Owen	Laidlaw	Balderstone	
Arnold	*Pate*	*Foster B*	*Matthews*	*Foster C*	*Bird*	*Lathan*	*Eccles*	*Clarke*	*Hodgson*	*McCaffrey*	

Mansfield make a lively start and Lathan forces a fine save from Ross. Soon after, Owen's shot on the turn from O'Neill's pass puts United ahead. Town press for the equaliser but the Carlisle defence, with Green and Spearritt outstanding, holds firm to frustrate the home side.

6 H FULHAM — 8/3 — 22 L — Att 21,570 2:12 — F-A 0-1 — H-T 0-0
Scorers: Barrett 67 — Ref: G Hill

1	2	3	4	5	6	7	8	9	10	11	12 sub used
Ross	Carr	Gorman	O'Neill	Green	Parker	Martin	Train	Owen	Laidlaw	Balderstone	Lloyd
Mellor	*Fraser*	*Strong*	*Mullery*	*Lacey*	*Moore*	*Dowie*	*Conway**	*Busby*	*Slough*	*Barrett*	

Carlisle's first ever cup quarter-final tie sees the home side take the game to Fulham as Mellor denies Laidlaw, Green and Owen. Busby has a chance after the break before Ross and Carr miss his centre and Barrett taps in. Finally Mellor thwarts O'Neill as Fulham hang on to their lead.

Home / Away table

#	Team	P	W	D	L	F	A	W	D	L	F	A	Pts
			Home					Away					
1	Derby Co	42	14	4	3	41	18	7	7	7	26	31	53
2	Liverpool	42	14	5	2	44	17	6	6	9	16	22	51
3	Ipswich T	42	17	2	2	47	14	6	3	12	19	30	51
4	Everton	42	10	9	2	33	19	6	6	9	23	30	50
5	Stoke C	42	12	7	2	40	18	5	8	8	24	30	49
6	Sheffield U	42	12	7	2	35	20	6	6	9	23	31	49
7	Middlesbro'	42	11	7	3	33	14	7	5	9	21	26	48
8	Manchester C	42	16	3	2	40	15	2	7	12	14	39	46
9	Leeds U	42	10	8	3	34	20	6	5	10	23	29	45
10	Burnley	42	11	6	4	40	29	6	5	10	28	38	45
11	QP Rangers	42	10	4	7	25	17	6	6	9	29	37	42
12	Wolves	42	12	5	4	43	21	2	6	13	14	33	39
13	West Ham U	42	10	6	5	38	22	3	7	11	20	37	39
14	Coventry C	42	8	9	4	31	27	4	6	11	20	35	39
15	Newcastle U	42	12	4	5	39	23	3	5	13	20	49	39
16	Arsenal	42	10	6	5	31	16	4	5	13	16	33	37
17	Birmingham C	42	10	4	7	34	28	4	5	12	19	33	37
18	Leicester C	42	8	7	6	25	17	4	5	12	21	43	36
19	Tottenham H	42	8	4	9	29	27	5	4	12	23	36	34
20	Luton T	42	8	6	7	27	26	5	5	13	20	39	33
21	Chelsea	42	4	9	8	22	31	5	6	10	20	41	33
22	CARLISLE U	42	8	2	11	22	21	4	3	14	21	38	29
		924	235	124	103	753	460	103	124	235	460	753	924

Odds & ends

Double wins: (1) Everton.

Double defeats: (8) Stoke C, Newcastle U, Luton T, Liverpool, Sheff U, QPR, Leeds U, West Ham U.

Won from behind: (1) Everton (a).

Lost from in front: (3) Leeds U (h), Burnley (a), Luton (h).

High spots: Winning the first three games of the season.
Topping the League on 20 August and from 24 to 27 August.
Playing in a higher division than Manchester U.
Reaching the quarter-finals of the FA Cup for the first and only time.

Low spots: Falling from top in August to the bottom by February.
Twice losing six League games in a row.
Elimination from both cup competitions by lower division clubs.
Losing six games to goals scored in the last five minutes.

Ever presents: (3) Bill Green, Bobby Parker, Ray Train.

Hat-tricks: None.

Hat-tricks against: (1) Terry Conroy (Stoke).

Leading scorer: Joe Laidlaw (16).

Appearances / Goals

Player	Appearances Lge	Sub	LC	Sub	FAC	Sub	Goals Lge	LC	FAC	Tot
Balderstone, Chris	27	4	1	2			1			1
Barry, Mike	8	4		1			1			1
Carr, Peter	39		2	3			1			1
Clarke, Frank	30	2	2	2			4		1	5
Clarke, Tom	9		1							
Gorman, John	30	1	2	3						
Green, Bill	42		2	4				1		1
Laidlaw, Joe	33	1	1	4			12		2	14
Martin, Dennis	37	1	1	3			7			7
McCartney, Mike	1	1								
McIlmoyle, Hugh	15	3	1				2			2
O'Neill, Les	36	1	1	4			8	1		9
Owen, Bobby	19	4	1	4			3		2	5
Parker, Bobby	42		2	4			1			1
Prudham, Eddie	5	1								
Ross, Allan	33			4			1			1
Spearritt, Eddie	13	1	1	2						
Train, Ray	42		2	4			2			2
Winstanley, Graham	1		1							
19 players used	462	23		44			43	1	5	49

SUBSCRIBERS AND VOTES FOR FAVOURITE CARLISLE PLAYER 1974-75

SUBSCRIBER	PLAYER
David J Altham	John Gorman
David Baker	Hugh McIlmoyle
Elizabeth Bouteba	Hugh McIlmoyle
Hannah Bouteba	John Gorman
Miriam Bouteba	Chris Balderstone
Saadi Bouteba	Ray Train
Denis Easterby	Chris Balderstone
Jane Ferguson	Chris Balderstone
John Ferguson	Chris Balderstone
Jason Garrick	George McVitie
David A Gibson	Allan Ross
Gladys Gibson	Les O'Neill
Nick Hadkiss	
John J Holliday	John Gorman
Ian Irving	Joe Laidlaw
Winnie Irving	Chris Balderstone
John Littlefair	Chris Balderstone
Neil Marshall	Chris Balderstone
Ian Niele	
Martin Roberts	Allan Ross
John Robertson	Ray Train
David Routledge	Chris Balderstone
Tony Rymer	
David John Saul	Chris Balderstone
Don Saul	Chris Balderstone
Warwick Sloan	Chris Balderstone
Tony Smith	Bobby Parker
Isabel & David Southward	Allan Ross
Joyce Steele	Allan Ross
Rachel Steele	Hugh McIlmoyle
Richard Studholme	Hugh McIlmoyle
Gail Thompson	Chris Balderstone
Mike Thompson	Dennis Martin
Colin Tickner	Hugh McIlmoyle
Don Tolson	Chris Balderstone